THE CHARACTER OF A MAN

THE CHARACTER OF A MAN

Reflecting the Image of Jesus

BRUCE MARCHIANO

HOWARD BOOKS
A DIVISION OF SIMON & SCHUSTER
NEW YORK LONDON TORONTO SIDNEY

Our purpose at Howard Books is to:
- *Increase faith* in the hearts of growing Christians
- *Inspire holiness* in the lives of believers
- *Instill hope* in the hearts of struggling people everywhere

Because He's coming again!

Published by Howard Books, a division of Simon & Schuster
1230 Avenue of the Americas, New York, NY 10020

The Character of a Man © 2006 by Bruce Marchiano

Library of Congress Cataloging-in-Publication Data

Marchiano, Bruce.
   The character of a man : reflecting the image of Jesus / Bruce Marchiano.
     p.cm.
  ISBN 1-58229-494-1
  1. Men (Christian theology) 2. Jesus Christ—Example. 3. Character—Religious aspects—Christianity. I. Title.

BT703.5.M34 2006
232.9'04—dc22

2006041114

10 9 8 7 6 5 4 3 2

ISBN 978-1-4516-2379-6

Manufactured in the United States of America

For information regarding special discounts for bulk purchases, please contact Simon & Schuster Special Sales at 1-800-456-6798 or business@simonandschuster.com.

Edited by Michele Buckingham
Interior design by John Mark Luke Designs
Cover design by Design Works Group
Cover illustration by Gaylon Wampler

To Dad and Mom, *thank you*.

And to Howard Publishing for their
unique support as together we

"fix our eyes on Jesus."

Contents

*"My heart is stirred
by a noble theme"* —
Jesus, Jesus, Jesus!

Discovering Jesus, the Man

It was several years ago that I, as an actor, enjoyed the breath-taking privilege of portraying Jesus on film in *The Gospel of Matthew*. I'd been born again for two years and was well on my way to an exciting journey in salvation. I was enjoying life with the Spirit of God growing (hopefully!) inside me. I was freed from sin, well aware of it, and learning more and more how to walk in the righteousness Jesus bought for me with His death and resurrection. Glory to His blessed Name!

Then the opportunity came to play Him—w*ow!* As a professional actor, I'd played many characters before, from a cop to a boxing promoter to a journalist to a gentle ex-con whose home was the backseat of a '63 Rambler (doesn't *that* sound wonderful?). But then I met a born-again director gearing up to put the Gospel of Matthew on film word for word. Over lunch at the downtown Los Angeles Hilton, he said to me, "You're the one," and the rest is history.

The next thing I knew, I had a beard on my face, sandals

on my feet, and I was "walking through" the most significant events in universal history—through the life of Jesus, the most significant *Man* in universal history. Though I couldn't have guessed it at the time, life for Bruce Marchiano as Bruce Marchiano knew it to be would never, ever be the same. And again, glory to Jesus!

Why do I bring up this life-changing opportunity—this personal "encounter" with the life of Jesus? Why do I make a special point of that word, *Man*? And what do these things have to do with the chapters and words that follow?

When a guy "acts" another person—and I can only speak for myself as an actor and the specific way that I trained as an actor—what he essentially does is tiptoe into another life. He walks a mile in another person's shoes. As best he can, he takes on another person's priorities, motivations, point of view, and desires. He does his best to understand and move into this other person's *heart*.

One of my lines in *Matthew* was Jesus's saying, "Out of the overflow of the heart the mouth speaks" (Matthew 12:34). Another was, "A tree is recognized by its fruit" (Matthew 12:33). Well surprise, surprise—there's an acting tenet that says, "A man's heart is reflected in his choices and actions." In other words, if I want to understand a man, all I have to do is look at his choices—what he does and how he does it—and I'll quickly understand what's in his heart. (I guess you could call it the gospel according to Stanislavski.)

So as an actor faced with the overwhelming, humbling, responsibility of "acting" Jesus, I got on my face before Him. I buried my nose in His Word. I bought every book I could find about Him and began a quest to *know* Him. I pieced through His every choice and every action. I knocked the familiarity off His words and dove into the dynamics and human realities of His every Gospel encounter.

Within those dynamics and realities I asked, "Why did Jesus do what He did in this situation and not all these other things He could have done? Why did he say this specific thing using these specific words? Why did he react *this* way and not *that* way? Why, why, why?

"And what does all this tell me about *who Jesus was* two thousand years ago? What does it tell me about His heart and His person, His nature and His ways? In other words, what kind of a Person was Jesus two thousand years ago? What was He like *as a Man*—as He lived His daily life, faced His daily challenges, pursued His daily hopes and passions?

"And what were those hopes and passions? What was in His heart as opposed to what's in my heart, or anyone else's heart for that matter? I mean, *Jesus* was the most common male name in first-century Israel, yet His life was shockingly different from anyone who ever lived before or after Him. Where did those differences come from?"

At the bottom of all that asking and searching was one seminal question: "Who was this *Man* named Jesus?"

I can't begin to tell you what it's like to stand on a hillside surrounded by hundreds of people and belt out, "Blessed are the poor in spirit, for theirs is the kingdom of heaven" (Matthew 5:3). I don't have words to describe how it feels to get down in the dirt with a filthy beggar, pull him into a Jesus-embrace, and whisper in his ear, "Be clean!" (Matthew 8:3).

I remember one scene where I was standing in a boat, a one-hundred-degree sun beating down on me and a one-hundred-degree wind whipping at my robes. There were throngs lining the shore, and I remember the heartbreak that overcame me as I spoke the words of Jesus, "He who has ears, let him hear" (Matthew 13:9). Like never before, I was deeply aware of how many didn't have "ears," of how many more still don't "hear."

Then there was the day I "hung" on a cross. Reenacting the Cross is my most vivid memory. "*Eloi, Eloi, lama sabachthani?* . . . My God, my God, why have you forsaken me?*" (Matthew 27:46).

JESUS.

Through it all, if you'll allow me to phrase it this way, my mind was blown sky high. My breath was taken out of me. My heart was stopped and flipped up one side and down the other, bent and shaped and twisted and turned, formed and re-formed,

> torn down and reconstructed,
>> refreshed and renewed,
>>> enlightened and amazed.

I "met" Jesus like I never imagined anyone could. I discovered Him in ways and depths I never dreamed possible. I'm sure I'd heard it all before, but through this experience I truly began to "get it"—His goodness, His care, His passion for a sinner like me.

There was another discovery too—a discovery that had nothing to do with Jesus in relationship with me personally. It had nothing to do with values or principles or revelations of His Word. It had nothing to do with the gospel per se—the good and glorious news of a God whose kingdom is forgiveness and grace.

It was quite simply, and oh so breathtakingly, the discovery of *Him*—of who Jesus was two thousand years ago. It was an encounter with Jesus, *the Man*. It was a glimpse into His character, a peek into His person. It was a tiny, tiptoed journey through the wonder of His perfection in practical, day-to-day human attributes—*male* attributes—as that maleness was manifested in His daily life.

Again—maybe even more—my mind was blown sky

high. In Jesus I met a Man who was a Man like no other man has ever been or ever will be. I met faithfulness personified. I met walking, talking kindness and graciousness. I met goodness, strength, and conviction *alive*! I met

> the summit of humbleness,
>> the pinnacle of gentleness,
>>> the utter fulfillment of confidence and care.

I met a Man whose thick, calloused hands looked like ordinary hands, but oh, how His touch was anything but! I met a Man whose voice sounded like any ordinary voice, but oh, the truthfulness and passion that spilled from its tenor! I met a Man whose face was no different from any face in the crowd—"He had no beauty or majesty to attract us to him, nothing in his appearance that we should desire him" (Isaiah 53:2)—but oh, what you would have seen if you took the time to look deeply into His eyes!

I met a Man who literally was living, breathing manhood—*true* manhood. In the sum of His ways, I met true masculinity defined and personified. I met the perfection of masculinity, the model, the ideal, the bar, the standard. I met the most masculine Man who ever walked the planet—the Man named Jesus. Glory to His Name!

And in the process, if I can phrase it this way, whereas I'd loved Him before, now I "fell in love" with Him. I fell in love with this wonder of a Man who, completely aside from the largess of His deity, was just one incredibly wonderful Guy.

I was also very, *very* challenged. My understanding of masculinity was completely rewritten as I deeply realized who, as a man, Jesus desires me to be. In my behavior and priorities, in the ways I relate to people and the motivations of my heart, in what comes out of my mouth and what's behind my touch, in the choices I make and the desires that drive me, in my actions and reactions, in the deepest depths of my greatest longings and the highest heights of my hopes and dreams—I am to be like Him.

JESUS.

It was as if, for the first time in my life, I understood what a man truly is, and I could see a clear picture of the man I could be. Philippians 2:5: "Your attitude should be the same as that of Christ Jesus." Romans 8:29: "For those God foreknew he also predestined to be conformed to the likeness of his Son." Matthew 5:48: "Be perfect, therefore, as your heavenly Father is perfect." John 13:15: "I have set you an example that you should do as I have done for you."

It was as if Jesus were saying to me (and these are huge, *huge* words), "This is who I am—*and this is who you, too, can be!*" Praise the Name of Jesus!

That's what *The Character of a Man* is all about. It's a book singularly and solely about Jesus, *the Man*. It's a book about who He was as a Man—His character and personality, and most specifically, His *masculine* personality. It's a book that explores Him as a Man in the way He walked out His manhood. It's a book that establishes Him as the ultimate male role model—the living, breathing definition of what a man truly is.

The Character of a Man is intended for everyone—men, women, born again, not born again. I've tried to write broadly enough to speak to folks across the board, because if there's one thing that's certain, it's that all of us—men and women, young and old, believer and unbeliever alike—*so* need to know and understand Him more and more. Oh, how we need to deeply, *deeply* know Jesus!

At the same time, *The Character of a Man* specifically invites those of us who are men to stop being "just guys" and start being Jesus. It lays before us a road map of character—*His* character. It opens the door to Jesus in us, operating through us, shaking our male trees free of the dead leaves and weak limbs of less-than-manly ways.

It wakes us up and challenges us to pursue being Him, living Him, shedding all that isn't Him, dressing ourselves as Him. It calls us to rise in the

> confidence,
>> peace,
>>> and sureness

that are available to all of us in and through Him.

It invites us, ultimately, to be fountains of Him, filled with Him, to "spill" Him through our manner and person into all the lives and relationships He's so graciously placed around us—our wives or sweethearts, our sons and daughters, our partners and friends, our parents and coworkers. Again, "This is who I am," Jesus says through the pages that follow, "and this is who you, too, can be!"

So come—let's discover Jesus. Let's explore who Jesus was two thousand years ago. Let's meet Him afresh and fall in love with Him anew. And for those of us who are men, let's discover what His manhood looks like. He was, and is, the perfection of a Man. Let's surrender our understanding of masculinity to the living God for a holy rewrite and overhaul. Let's discover what "masculine" *truly* means. Come, let's discover Jesus!

May I pray:

Dear Lord, oh Lord, how our hearts yearn for You! At the end of everything we can choose to chase in this world —good things, even—there is You. Yes, Lord, we just need You.

So we gather through the pages of this book, Lord, to find and discover You at deeper levels than ever before.

Oh, how that brings a smile to Your heavenly face!

And we know You are a God who rewards those who seek You. You respond with waterfalls of refreshing and understanding, guidance and care, healing and wholeness, purpose and value, focus and confidence, joy and fruitfulness. You respond with all the "goodnesses" that are You.

Lord Jesus, begin even now to reveal Yourself in all the fullness of who You are—as a Man. Reach into our hearts and lives and touch us with Your love. Gird us up by Your righteous right hand and build us, Lord—build us into You! Come, Lord Jesus, come!

In the precious Name of Jesus, I pray. Amen and amen.

A MAN OF EXCELLENCE

"You are the most excellent of men." These are words from Psalm 45 that describe Jesus—penned, interestingly enough, centuries before He was ever born.

The psalm goes on to describe Him even more: "Your lips have been anointed with grace." "God has blessed you forever." "A scepter of justice will be the scepter of your kingdom." "You love righteousness and hate wickedness." "All your robes are fragrant with myrrh and aloes and cassia." "Daughters of kings are among your honored women." "God, your God, has set you above your companions by anointing you with the oil of joy."

The writer of Psalm 45 introduces all these verses of Spirit-inspired wonder with a simple, most breathtaking declaration: "My heart is stirred by a noble theme"—*Jesus*.

Grace, justice, righteousness.

Honor, nobility, joy.

Manhood, manliness, masculinity.

It is an interesting reality that Jesus is rarely, if ever, thought of as "a man," if you know what I mean. One never hears His Name in discussions of masculinity. There are many male role models, both ancient and contemporary, but for some odd reason, He's rarely on the list.

Sure, we hear about Christlikeness and about modeling Christ's love and forgiveness. But I'm talking about being a man. You know—a *man*. Why is Jesus never thought of like that?

I'm going to guess there are many reasons. For one, as much as we may know, know, know that "the Word became flesh" (John 1:14), deep inside we still tend to carry this sense of Jesus's being, well, not quite 100 percent flesh. The evidence of this is all the lofty and glamorized artistic representations we see that, as real as any of them get, never quite get *that* real. Perhaps it's His bluer-than-blue eyes or His perfectly combed hair. Maybe it's His graceful stance or His always-looking-upward gaze. As talented and well-intentioned as any artist may be, there's always *something* that distracts from His humanness.

Religious formality and tradition, I'm guessing, also play a role. Whether that takes the form of "thee, thou, and thine" kinds of presentations or the kinds with bright suits and lots of shouting, the sense one gets of Jesus is still the same—just a little "nonreal."

It's also a very big pill for us to deeply, fully swallow—that God became *just like you and me.* That's not to say we don't believe it; it's just that its base reality is so far beyond remarkable, it doesn't entirely fit into our limited, human understanding.

But the truth is, if you could have sat across the table from Jesus and shared a meal with Him two thousand years ago, you would have noticed nothing unique or extraordinary about Him. "He grew up before him like a tender shoot, and like a root out of dry ground. He had no beauty or majesty to attract us to him, nothing in his appearance that we should desire him" (Isaiah 53:2). In His humanity, Jesus was given no advantages over you and me, and indeed, He chose to take none.

JESUS.

To paint a perfectly accurate painting of Jesus, in fact, or make a perfectly accurate Jesus film, one would have to paint or film Him in such a way that you and I couldn't pick Him out in a crowd. There would just be a sea of first-century faces in a marketplace or wherever, and somewhere in the middle of them all, dressed entirely the same, indistinguishable from anyone else, would be Jesus—a Man named Jesus.

Why do we struggle to see Him so? There is another reason:

the problem of masculinity and our common perceptions of what that word truly means. Say the word *masculine* and what generally comes to mind? Tough talk and football players. Hummers and Harleys.

"Hit back and hit hard."
"Take no prisoners."
"Never say die."

Though we may admire them as qualities, we tend not to think of grace as masculine or kindness as macho. When was the last time you heard talk of compassion or tenderness in relation to strength? When was the last time you heard someone say that doing nothing while people spit in your face is the manly thing to do?

Yes, deep inside, as much as we know it isn't so, we tend to see those wonderful qualities of grace, kindness, compassion, tenderness, self-control—*the qualities of Jesus*—as not *really* masculine.

Again, the evidence is in so much artistic representation, whether visual or literary. How often—how tragically often —have we seen Jesus portrayed as more of a "pious pansy" than anything else: rosy cheeks, gleaming white hands, silken robes, aloof and above it all? Imagine His voice, and one tends to think "Shakespeare." Picture His clothes, and one tends to think "white." Think of His stature, and one immediately thinks "slender." Oh, how far from truth can nontruth be!

Two thousand years ago, Jesus was a Man. I mean, *a Man*. He walked the alleyways and marketplaces of ancient Israel, the living God in a living Man, two feet as firmly on the ground as two feet have ever been on the ground—even more so.

He was born in a first-century barn, probably a cave. Of course, that's not what makes a man a man, but in pursuit of an accurate representation of *the Man*, it certainly presents a picture that's anything but soft. It certainly displays a reality that's far from glorious, far from advantaged, and far *below* above it all. In fact, it's a reality that's miles below the-same-as-us-all. I don't know anyone who was born in a barn, and I would venture to guess that few, if any of us, do. *But Jesus was.*

JESUS.

Shaking free from our glamorized familiarity with the Nativity, it's a mind-exploding reality to consider. He was the Son of the living God. His Spirit-hands tossed the stars into the night sky. His words breathed life into all creation. He's the Alpha and Omega, the Glory of the Universe—*and He was born in a barn.*

There's nothing exalted about that. There's nothing lofty or religious or full of Christmas splendor. His first smell was animal manure. His first bed was the trough from which animals ate. It's so shockingly hard, so shockingly base, and so shockingly *real.*

As He grew, Jesus learned to work with His hands. He did blue-collar labor for most of His life. Again, physical work is not the measure of manhood, but it is a reality that has nothing to do with manicured perfection or soft, silken gowns. It's a reality that produces dirt under the fingernails, sweat, bruises, and scars. It molds tanned, sinewy, powerful arms. It sculpts thick legs and barrel shoulders, not creamy-smooth delicacy and slightness.

JESUS.

His ministry continued in the same vein. Page after page in Gospel after Gospel we see Jesus sleeping in open fields, walking from town to town, on His knees in the dirt—*hanging from a tree*! Two thousand years ago Jesus said, "Foxes have holes and birds of the air have nests, but the Son of Man has no place to lay his head" (Matthew 8:20). He was the Son of the living God—the Creator of everything that was ever created—*and He had nowhere to lay His head.*

Again, that's a hard reality. It's a down-and-dirty reality. Oh, we look back in religious composure and scriptural sophistication and say, "Of course." But when we strip away all the familiarity and push ourselves to look at it in its raw actuality, it's so *shocking*.

Jesus was a Man who had *all the power of the universe and then some* at His fingertips. He opened blind eyes. He fed thousands with a single prayer. He effortlessly resurrected people from the dead. Oh, how our familiar acquaintance with these events robs us of cutting-edge appreciation for how truly awesome they are!

Imagine you're sitting at a red light next to a cemetery and suddenly, out of the corner of your eye, you see it: the ground explodes, and out of the hole, *a man stands up*.

My goodness! How would any of us react to that? Our minds would explode. We'd come entirely unglued. We'd race around manically, hyperventilating, not knowing what to do. We'd probably be frightened out of our wits! And from that point on, *our lives would never be the same.* Glory to Jesus!

That's how it was two thousand years ago. *That's* the power and resources Jesus walked in. *That's* the bigness of the breath-stealing command that lay at His beck and call.

Jesus catapulted from the waters of His Jordan baptism, and like thunder, El Shaddai Himself belted from one end of the millennia to the other: "This is my Son, whom I love; with him I am well pleased" (Matthew 3:17). He was *His Son*, and He slept in the fields! H*e was the living Son of the living God*—and He had nowhere to lay His head! Oh, shocking, *shocking* reality!

JESUS!

Then the day came when He did "lay His head." He laid it back on a beam of wood. He laid it back against a mangle of thorns. He laid His head; they raised Him up. They did terrible things—unmentionable things. And He died.

*O my God, I cry out by day, but you do not answer. . . .
I am a worm and not a man. . . . Many bulls surround
me, strong bulls of Bashan encircle me. Roaring lions
tearing their prey open their mouths wide against me.
I am poured out like water, and all my bones are out
of joint. . . . My strength is dried up . . . my tongue
sticks to the roof of my mouth. . . . Dogs have
surrounded me; a band of evil men has encircled me,
they have pierced my hands and my feet.
—from Psalm 22*

JESUS.

*His appearance was so disfigured beyond that of any man
and his form marred beyond human likeness. . . .
He was despised and rejected by men, a man of sorrows,
and familiar with suffering. . . . He was led like a
lamb to the slaughter. . . . He was cut off from the
land of the living. . . . He was assigned a grave with
the wicked. . . . He poured out his life unto death.
—from Isaiah 52 and 53*

JESUS.

No, there was nothing "soft" about this Man two thousand years ago. There was nothing weak or unmanly. His was a reality that was as hard as reality can get—

   a sweat-in-the-sun,

      tears-in-the-dirt,

         blood-in-the-sand reality.

And in all that realness and authenticity He alone stood as "the most excellent of men."

   JESUS!

What would excellence look like in a man? How would perfection of masculinity play out? After all, Jesus was perfect in every way. He was the perfect reflection of His Father's image. He was the perfect fulfillment of the purpose for which He had been birthed. He was the perfection of righteousness and holiness, completely "without sin." (Hebrews 4:15). *And He was the perfection of character in a Man.*

Jesus alone perfectly became everything His Father ever meant for a man, manliness, and masculinity to be. Jesus was the "ultimate Man," if you will—the true, living definition of what truly is a man.

He lived every moment—every breath, every look, every touch—in 100 percent perfection of goodness, 100 percent in the bull's-eye of His Father's guidance and will. He lived 100 percent free of foolishness and folly, fear and unworthy considerations. Not even one millimeter of His masculine being was bruised by indulgence in sinful pursuits.

He lived every frame of His life in 100 percent magnificence of purpose and perfection of focus. He spent His talents and resources in a perfect economy of effort and activity, reaping a perfection of all the fruitfulness He was born to bear.

Can you imagine never wasting even a billionth of a second of your life? Can you imagine every move you make and every breath you take counting for the biggest "everything" of every life: eternal life?

JESUS!

Then there was His perfection of personality—His *male* personality. Can you even begin to wrap your mind around a Man who, just sitting there doing nothing, radiates

> wholeness and care,
>> loveliness and genuineness,
>>> strength and conviction,
>>>> calm and splendor?

His every word is 100 percent truth, 100 percent sureness. His every word overflows with healing and encouragement, blessing and kindness, certainty and might, hope and confidence. His every word breathes life and resurrection into the weariness of your heart.

There's never one hint of an ugly remark, never the tiniest escape of a sarcastic chuckle or a "just kidding" jest. "Your lips have been anointed with grace," the psalmist says of Him. Never once does He complain or moan. Never once does He cut you off or lash out because "I'm just a little tired today."

Can you imagine just hanging around with this Man, this living, breathing kingdom of God in human envelope? Can you imagine looking into His eyes and seeing 100 percent trustworthiness and faithfulness, no question about it? Can you imagine

perfection of joy;
    perfection of graciousness;
        perfection of peace,
            tenderness, courage, commitment?

Can you imagine dignity and nobility, honor and command, genuineness and ease, all in their highest ideal? Can you imagine "compassionate . . . slow to anger, abounding in love" (Exodus 34:6) right there before your eyes?

Psalm 27:4 whispers this phrase: "to gaze upon the beauty of the LORD." Can you imagine actually doing that? Can you imagine the fullness of that beauty—the perfection of beauty and all that true beauty means—dripping from the Presence and Person of a flesh-and-blood Man?

I have seen you in the sanctuary and
beheld your power and your glory.
—Psalm 63:2

Behold the beauty of the Lord! Behold the *Man!*

It's such a wonder to consider: two thousand years ago, the Son of the living God stepped into our very real world and lived a very real life. He was born a very real boy and given a very real name—one of the most common male names in first-century Israel: Jesus, Y'shua, Joshua, *"God saves."*

He grew into a very real Man. He earned a working man's living by the sweat of His very real brow. He went home each day with hunger in His belly and fatigue in His limbs. He sat with His family and He laughed and He cried. He pressed through all the difficulties, disappointments, and celebrations that human life in this imperfect world offers us all.

Then He leaped into ministry. He walked away from the comfort and security of home and family to sit in the synagogues of His beloved Israel, to stand on her street corners and pour His heart out. Then He laid down on a piece of wood and poured His heart out even more.

JESUS.

And through it all—through every parable and teaching, every miracle and rebuke, every "I love you" and every "Woe to you," through every bead of sweat that swelled on the surface of His nose, every tear that spilled over His cheeks, and every drop of blood that leaked from His wounds and stained Golgotha's sand beneath His dying feet—through it all, Jesus stood as the living revelation of the living God.

He was the human unveiling of God's character and God's ways—the character and ways He had come to display and make known.

Equally so, He was the living revelation of perfection in a living Man. He was the model, the definition—"the most excellent of men." He was the human unveiling of what "man-character" truly is. He was the personification of truly masculine ways.

"This is who I am," declared Jesus through

His every action and interaction,
　　His every choice and priority,
　　　　His every behavior and spoken word.

"And this is who you—oh, My Father's sons—this is who you can be!"

Jesus, Jesus, Jesus! Glory to the Name of Jesus!

Recently I was e-mailed a precious, precious story. It's kind of funny, but given the kinds of professional activities I'm involved in, if anything has to do with Jesus, people come running to me with it.

That's no complaint at all—I'm actually very thankful for it. In fact, a couple of nights ago I was watching an acting peer do an interview about his latest movie. I could tell that he was really striving to come up with something meaningful to say about the storyline and the character he played.

Deep inside, I think, we all crave real purpose. We all want to make some kind of "contribution to the world" somehow. We want to make a "difference." I know a lot of writers, filmmakers, musicians, and artists are like that.

So here was this actor trying hard to come up with something of significance to say. But you can't squeeze water from a rock. At the end of the day, his movie was just another silly movie, no different from a million other silly movies. It was just popcorn entertainment meant to "keep the people smiling." The character he played was less than remarkable too: an alcoholic lawyer going through a divorce (how enthralling!).

It was sad, but no matter how hard this guy tried, there was nothing interesting—let alone "change the world" significant—that he could talk about. So the interviewer made a few silly jokes, and that was that.

For me, though, that wasn't that. As I watched, I had a sudden moment of enlightenment. The thought hit me: *Here's this guy struggling to come up with something important to say—and look at what God has given me to talk about! I get to talk about Jesus, the most important Importance in the universe!*

Truly, it was a moment that sent me to my knees in thanksgiving. Everything around me is just Jesus, Jesus, Jesus. He did that, and I couldn't be more thrilled. Glory to the Name of Jesus!

Now to the story . . .

Several business partners, it seems, were racing along the

sidewalks of Manhattan on their way to the biggest meeting of their lives. It was the meeting they'd scratched tooth and nail to secure, the meeting they'd dreamed of and aimed for from day one of their partnership. They'd spent endless hours in preparation and planning, research and strategizing. If the deal went through, their business lives would go from "zero to sixty" in one six- or maybe even seven-figure "sign on the dotted line."

I don't know how many partners there were—four or five, let's say. The New York streets were typically elbow to elbow, so they did their best to hurry along, bobbing and weaving through the crowd and ducking and diving across traffic. They looked at their watches and really began to burn rubber. Finally they whipped around the last corner that would take them to the front door of the office building where their meeting was being held.

But as fate and the reality of big city streets would have it, a vendor with a snack cart was stationed just around that corner. The businessmen made the turn and were taken totally by surprise. They slammed into the cart, toppling it and sending sandwiches, potato chips, fruit, and peanuts flying in every direction. The vendor, a young woman, was knocked flat. It was a total wipeout.

Well, the businessmen were already late, and the collision only made them later. So they leaped to their feet and knocked the soil off their seven-hundred-dollar suits as best they could. A few of them barked some choice words at the laid-out vendor: "Are you nuts, setting up a cart around a corner like that?" "What's wrong with you?" "Get that thing out of here, for crying out loud!" (I know, I know . . . *guys.*)

Finally recomposed, the partners bolted into the office building and headed for the elevators and the fifty-third floor. That is, all but one.

"Go on without me," this one guy told his partners. The other businessmen were stunned. "Are you nuts?" "What's wrong with you?" "This is the really big one, for crying out loud!" But he stood his ground. He wasn't going anywhere. His partners finally turned and rushed into the building without him.

The man returned to the scene of the accident to help the vendor. It turned out she was a blind immigrant girl—just a kid, really—doing what she could to make a buck. How disoriented and scared she must have been! Can you fathom not being able to see in a circumstance like that? Her surroundings had been totally reshuffled. Nothing was where it should be anymore. And all the people—she could hear them all around her, the footsteps, the noise. Who were they? Where were they? Would anyone stop and help? Can you imagine her confusion and fear?

Another fear gripped her heart too: What would her boss

do when he found out what happened? Would he make her pay for the damage to the cart, for all the food that was lost? How *could* she pay for it all?

The businessman set his briefcase down and reached to lift the girl to her feet. He calmed her and told her he was sorry. He assured her that he would gather everything and set her cart back up for her, just like new. He even walked over to another vendor and bought her a bottle of cold water. He kept talking to her, calmly settling her, all the while picking up her sandwiches and peanuts and chips and promising he would pay for everything that was spoiled.

Here was this man who had aimed his efforts for years toward a specific opportunity. No doubt he'd dreamed and dreamed of this day, talking about it with friends over endless cups of coffee, sitting at his computer late into the night. Hundreds of thousands of dollars were potentially his to be made on the fifty-third floor—and here he was on the sidewalk, taking the time to care for the immigrant girl.

When he finished resetting and restocking the cart, he asked her again if she was OK. She nodded that she was. He cuffed her shoulder, bought one of her sandwiches, apologized again, and turned to go on his way.

"Excuse me, sir!" she cried as she reached for his arm to stop him, her blind gaze fixed blankly over his shoulder. "Are you Jesus? *You're just like Jesus . . .*"

A man takes the time to care. A man sets himself aside no matter the cost, does the "right thing," and looks far, far, far beyond his own little world. He moves in compassion and giving. He moves in kindness and grace. He moves in integrity and principle. He blesses and blesses. And the world around him—every life that lives in his home, every life that works next to him in the office or factory, every life that crosses his path as he goes about living day by day—looks at that man and thinks *Jesus*.

He was the perfection of manhood—"the most excellent of men."

JESUS!

Glory to the Name of Jesus!

A MAN OF HUMILITY

To look into Jesus's eyes two thousand years ago was to look into the eyes of living humbleness. To sit by His side was to rub shoulders with its human presence. To stand in a meadow or on a hillside and listen to His voice was to hear its divine heartbeat. To feel His touch was to experience its holiness, its warmth, its ease.

Jesus *was* humbleness two thousand years ago. The word could easily have been His name. He lived it and breathed it. He baptized Himself in it and revealed His Person through it.

It hung as His hallmark. It lay at the foot of His male foundation. As He coursed through the alleyways and marketplaces of ancient Israel, it stood among the cornerstone qualities that defined Him as a Man—and may well be the quality that defined Him most.

It was at the root of His excellence and the core of His masculinity. It was *who He was* in personality two thousand years ago, the nutshell of His nature and the current of His character.

It was His chosen lifestyle. It was who He taught the people to be, and who He longed for them to understand and accept Him to be.

Humility. Humbleness. "Taking the very nature of a servant," He *"made himself nothing"* (Philippians 2:7).

JESUS.

It is a startling reality that God would reveal Himself this way, that Jesus would be that kind of Man. If it doesn't strike us as startling, that's only because we're so familiar with the story. It's only because we view it in hindsight.

The rough edges and emotional punch of the Gospels fall victim to highbrow words like *propitiation* and studies that fill us with valuable head knowledge but leave us starved for heart understanding. Scripture phrases such as "laid in a manger" and "man of sorrows" should boggle our minds, but for some reason they more commonly ring as religious clichés.

Two thousand years ago, however, that was not so. Eye to eye with Jesus—eyewitness to who He was and how that played out in His day-to-day life—there was nothing cliché. His was not a "religious" reality, if I can put it that way. It was a *human* reality. What the people saw two thousand years ago, and walked alongside, and talked with, and worked next to, and ate meals with, and watched from a distance, was a living, breathing Man—a Man with a shockingly different manner and shockingly different ways.

I'm convinced that's one of the huge reasons that people

largely rejected Him. He was just *so* against the grain, so completely the opposite of who people expected Him to be—dare I say, who people *wanted* Him to be.

A story in John chapter 7 tells it all. It is a wide-open window into how absolutely baffling the people found this Man, Jesus . . .

It's the Feast of Tabernacles, and the whole of the ancient world is trekking to Jerusalem to enjoy a time of vacation and worship. Jesus has been doing miracles left and miracles right. The buzz about Him stretches up and down the length of Israel, and He is fast becoming "all the rage."

So there Jesus is, wandering through the small villages of Galilee, doing His ministry thing and spending time with family. His brothers can't wait to go up to the Feast, and they begin packing and preparing. Conspicuously, though, Jesus isn't preparing. He just keeps right on doing what He's doing. He keeps right on preaching in the small-town synagogues and on the small-town street corners, reaching out to the small-town people and healing their small-town diseases.

His brothers don't get it. They approach Jesus, and you can hear their frustration as they confront Him: "You ought to leave here and go to Judea, so that your disciples may see the miracles you do. *No one who wants to become a public figure acts in secret*" (John 7:3–4).

At first glance we may want to shake our heads at those brothers for what seems like blind ignorance. But again, we're looking back on the story in the context of our religious understanding and belief. Let's instead look at it from *their* perspective. Let's "walk that mile" in their shoes and place ourselves in their immediate reality.

These guys have a brother who spits in the sand and a man's blind eyes pop open. He thanks God for a few scraps of food, and those scraps explode into five thousand fish sandwiches. He whispers two words to a dead girl and she stands right up. It's so far beyond mind-blowing that it's, well, mind-blowing!

Talk about "talent"! Talk about a guy with "potential"! Talk about someone who could rise higher than any man ever rose, own more than any man ever owned, dominate and possess beyond what any man ever dreamed of dominating and possessing!

Talk about a man for whom "the sky's the limit"! And that cliché doesn't begin to draw a picture of even a corner of His capacity. After all, He's the Guy who created the sky! Its vastness and glory is but a pitiful puddle within the shadow of a peck-measure of His limit—which is nothing short of limitless. Glory to Jesus!

But what does "Big Brother" do with all this gifting, resource, and ability? He sits on street corners and talks to beggars. He wanders from no-name town to no-name town, hanging out with no-name people. He spends night after night alone on the mountaintops; He says it's because He has to pray.

He raises from the dead the nobody son of a nobody widow. He even raises the slave of (spit to say the word) a Roman centurion. And mind-bending foolishness upon mind-bending foolishness, He asks for nothing—no pay, *nothing*—to do it. He could ask for millions for His services, but instead He asks for nothing.

JESUS.

How would most if not all of us react to a brother who acted like that? Think of it this way: Your brother has a voice that would shame Pavoratti, Bocelli, Sinatra, and Josh Groban combined. He has offers from every agency and record company in America. He could sell out Carnegie Hall a hundred times over. Every TV network is offering him a blank check to headline a prime-time special. Every magazine in the country, *Good Morning America*, *Oprah*, *The Tonight Show*—they're all begging him for an interview. Across the nation, he is the one everyone is talking about.

But he says no to it all. He prefers to sing in homeless shelters. He stands on street corners and doesn't even put out a tin cup. There will be no Web site, no CDs. He avoids New York and L.A. but turns up in towns like McGrawsville,

Indiana. He could easily make billions, but he takes a job washing dishes in a diner instead.

Getting the picture? It's a picture of Jesus.

Let me draw another illustration, except this time it's *your son*. He's the greatest baseball phenom to ever step onto a field. He's so far above and beyond anyone who ever played the game, it isn't funny. As a Little Leaguer, he was throwing 150-mile-an-hour fastballs. Today at seventeen he's throwing effortlessly at 260—a perfect strike every pitch. In fact he's never thrown less than a perfect game. From the time he was eight years old until now, not one hitter has ever even been able to get the bat off his shoulder, let alone connect with one of your son's pitches.

So, of course, every major-league team has offered your son a blank check. He could name his salary—one hundred million dollars a year for the rest of his life. Nike, Adidas, and Reebok have offered him endorsement deals for another hundred mil. Ford, Chevrolet, Nissan—they'll give him anything he wants to do a commercial. *Sports Illustrated* wants to make him athlete not just of the year but of the century—the millennium! I mean, the opportunities are endless. All your son has to do is say one simple word: "yes."

But he won't. He won't say yes to major-league baseball, to interviews, or endorsements. He turns down every award and shies away from every accolade. He won't even say yes to a college scholarship. He just won't say yes to any of it.

In fact, every time they want to "make him king" (John 6:15), he slips away where no one can find him. All he wants to do is volunteer in the local convalescent home. All he wants to do is clean bed pans and wash old people's feet for no pay. When you confront him about his wasted opportunities, he just smiles and says, "I have food to eat that you know nothing about" (John 4:32). How ridiculous an answer is that? How bizarre, mind-boggling, and even downright disappointing can a son's behavior get?

Let's be deep-down honest: Most all of us would probably send that son to every counselor we could find. We would fast and pray and cry out to God for him. We would call all our friends and say, "Please pray for my Junior! He's throwing his life away!"

We might also tell him he's disobeying God and not being a "good steward." We might say, "God has given you an incredible talent. He's given you gifting He has never given to anyone in history. How can you toss it away? If you *really* want to help old people, then go for the money and fame, and use it to build homes for the elderly and provide medicine and programs . . ."

Yes, as much as any one of us might love this son and try to respect his choices, the best of us would have a tough time wrapping our understanding around his behavior.

Welcome to Jesus.

"But Bruce, Jesus was in ministry." Amen! Can you imagine

a guy in ministry saying no to a feature in *Christianity Today* or *Charisma*? Let's say *The 700 Club* calls and says, "We want to focus an entire program on you and the work you're doing." Can you imagine a minister saying, "Thank you, but no"?

Is there a Christian writer (myself included) who wouldn't want to have a *New York Times* bestseller? Is there a CCM artist who *doesn't* want to receive a Dove Award? Of course not! Such opportunities are blessings all the way around. In righteousness they're hoped for, prayed for, and sought after. They mean national exposure; they mean success. In one fell swoop they can put a ministry or a singer or a writer "on the map."

Then there's Jesus two thousand years ago, who thinks and conducts His life in ways that are vastly different from ours (Isaiah 55:8). There's Jesus who actually avoids "the map." There's Jesus who hides from national exposure and turns away from personal success.

His brothers hit the nail straight on the head when they say, "No one who wants to become a public figure acts in secret." Jesus isn't interested in people's attention—*Jesus is interested in people*. The focus of His ambition is clear, pure, and oh so simple:

> His heavenly Father,
>> His Father's kingdom,
>>> and His Father's people.

Glory to His amazing Name!

And so He serves. As incomprehensible as it truly is, of all the different "natures" the Son of the living God could have dressed Himself in, He chooses the lowliest nature there is: the nature of a servant (Philippians 2:7). He humbles Himself (v. 8). He asks for nothing; He receives nothing. He just rolls up His sleeves and gets down in the streets with forgotten, rejected, bruised, and battered people—*and He serves.*

"You're blind? Let me open your eyes." "You're deaf? Here are new ears." "You're crippled? I give you legs." "You're hungry? Come and eat." "You're misled? Here's the truth." "You're dead? Rise and live!"

And surpassing all of the above: "You're born condemned?" "Here's My life."

JESUS.

And through it all, not even once does He serve Himself—*not once.* It is a breath-stealing, eye-opening reality. It is a gaping, shocking window into the absolute depth of the Man's humility,

the completeness of His commitment,
the quality of His character,
the heartbeat of His soul.

There isn't one story in Matthew, Mark, Luke, or John in which Jesus uses any of His power or resources for Himself. One hundred percent of the time He does only one thing with all that He is: *He gives it away*. To the glory of His Father, He serves people. He gives it all away.

My goodness! It's so far beyond our most far-reaching understanding of "good." It's so shockingly shattering of our most righteous definitions of what "masculine good" really looks like.

As a Man, Jesus possesses the ability to feed five thousand people with a single prayer, but for Himself He *chooses* to buy food like the rest of us (John 4:8). Diseases vanish at the whisper of His voice, yet He provides for Himself "no place to lay His head" (Matthew 8:20). He transfigures supernaturally alongside Moses and Elijah, crossing back and forth between heaven and earth, yet He makes a living by the sweat of His brow, sawing wood and hammering nails.

This is a Man who has the power to raise people from the dead, yet this is a Man who walks everywhere He goes. He doesn't "zap" Himself a horse to ride—and I know that sounds funny, but we must never forget: *this Man is God*. If anyone has the right to do a thing like that, it's Him. In fact, if you really think about it, it's even funnier that He doesn't do it. *He's God!* If you and I had that power and those resources, wouldn't we use them for our own purposes and comfort?

But therein lies the difference between Jesus and—well, me. He doesn't even take five bucks out of the money sack to hire a carriage. There isn't one moment of "I'm entitled to this." Of course, one time He rides a donkey (*ahem, ahem*), but except for that one instance, like the poorest of peasants, He walks. He buys His own food. He sleeps in the fields.

JESUS.

I can imagine people two thousand years ago being a little confused by that—maybe a lot confused, really. I can imagine one of the apostles pulling Jesus aside and saying something like, "Master, I've got some ideas that I think can help the ministry. You're Messiah, but no one is respecting You like they ought to. I think if You dressed a little nicer and maybe had a house in the nice section of Jerusalem—nothing too fancy, just something befitting a Messiah—then people would pay better attention.

"Oh, and this thing you have for walking everywhere we—oops, I mean You, go. Forgive me, Master, but it's just not a good witness. You should have a chariot that makes a Messiah statement. Not only do You deserve it, but it would take days off of our traveling time, and we could reach so many more people . . ."

Unfortunately, those kinds of considerations are typical in ministry circles today, and when it comes to human wisdom and human ways, people two thousand years ago thought no differently than people think today.

In Matthew 20:20–28, for example, we see the apostles vying for who will sit at Jesus's right and left in His kingdom. We look back at the guys and kind of chuckle about it, but how often do we hear similar talk today? "I want lots of jewels in my heavenly crown, Brother!" "He-e-e-e-y, the Lord's building you a *big* mansion in glory!" Nothing much has changed.

Here are these guys in their standard guy nature, wanting and wanting—and here's Jesus in His breathtaking Jesus nature, giving and giving. Here are these guys aiming for the same things most all of us aim for—privilege and position—and here's Jesus, tossing every privilege of His position away. Here are these guys thinking a man and a man's success are one seamless thing, and here's Jesus, *the living Truth of what a Man and a Man's success truly are.*

I can only imagine the look on His ever-understanding face as He pleads with them to "get it": "Whoever wants to become great among you must be your servant, and whoever wants to be first must be your slave" (Matthew 20:26–27). In other words, it's all about serving, guys—the complete opposite of what you might think.

Kingdom life,
    kingdom character,
        peak masculinity,
            pinnacle success—

it's all about humbling yourself before your Father and humbling yourself before everyone around you.

It's all about taking that backseat so that others may sit in the front. It's all about turning away from the crowns men typically seek and offering them to others who may deserve them less. "Whoever exalts himself will be humbled, and whoever humbles himself will be exalted" (Matthew 23:12). It's all about giving, guys. It's all about dying to self and giving yourself away.

Then He goes on, as the ultimate Man, to "define" Himself, and in so doing, He declares the ultimate of what every man can be: "Just as the Son of Man *did not come to be served, but to serve, and to give His life* as a ransom for many" (Matthew 20:28).

Wow, what a head-on collision with human nature! Two thousand years down the line, you and I read those scriptures and no doubt get a tiny taste of how those words must have rung in the apostles' ears that day. Oh, how entirely challenging! Oh, how grating against my every male instinct! Oh, how the mind so immediately goes to rationalizing away the clear, unmistakable, unqualified black-and-whiteness of His words:

"must be your servant,"

"must be your slave,"

"not to be served,"

"serve . . . give . . . slave."

"No, no, please Lord, *no!*" we cry. "Isn't it true that 'he who dies with the most toys wins'? Surely competitiveness, getting ahead, increase, and championship are the orders of the day! Pretty girls and BMWs, big motorcycles and even bigger trucks, Rolex watches and Mont Blanc pens, a first-class upgrade and a plasma TV, a leather jacket and a Nike logo, a seat on the fifty-yard line and a son who's the star of the team—surely this is the stuff of real manhood. These are the hallmarks of a guy who's 'arrived.'

"And about that *slave* word, Lord. You're kidding me, right? (Hold on—let me look in my concordance for alternate interpretations.) A slave is the last thing anyone wants to be. It's the lowest rung on the human ladder. It's a human nothing. (Wait a minute . . . why does that sound so familiar? Where have I heard it before?) Surely Lord, when You say, 'slave,' You don't really mean, well, *'slave.'*"

But He did say "slave," and just in case anyone doubted then or doubts today that that's exactly what He meant, one afternoon He modeled it for us all by bleeding in the sand and hanging on a tree.

After all, what is a slave? Someone who does all your work for you, and it costs you nothing. What was Jesus doing on that cross that day? He was doing all of my work for me—of righteousness. And what did it cost me? *Nothing.* It was, and is, the *free gift* of

> forgiveness,
>> righteousness,
>>> and eternal life.

Yes, Jesus didn't just love you and me. Jesus didn't just save you and me. Jesus, the Son of the living God, the Alpha and Omega in a human envelope, made Himself *our slave*. He literally and entirely *"gave Himself away."*

JESUS.

Stripped of religious dressing, such bare truth can be understandably uncomfortable. But I think of the apostle John's Last Supper account of Jesus's actions, beginning with the breath-stealing words of John 13:1: *"He now showed them the full extent of his love."* What does Jesus do? He gets down on the floor and washes everyone's feet. He tears a piece of bread, saying, "This is my body." He pours out wine, saying, "This is my blood." He encourages them, "Remain in my love." Then He walks out the door and submits Himself to all of hell's hand. He humbles Himself *before you and me*.

JESUS.

I think, too, of another story that captures the breathtaking quality of Jesus's humbleness, the depth and totality of His selflessness. Jesus stands on a hillside before a Galilean throng, holding five loaves of bread and two fish. We all know the story: Jesus miraculously multiplies the loaves and the fish so that thousands can eat.

But there's a little detail that's mentioned in the Gospel accounts—a detail that rarely receives attention. Yet it very well could be the most profound and life-changing element in the entire story, if only we would allow it to sink deep into our human hearts: "Taking the five loaves and the two fish and looking up to heaven, *he gave thanks*" (Matthew 14:19).

Here is the Son of the living God, the Everlasting unto Everlasting, holding in His hands what most folks would consider mere scraps, what no one would consider prosperity, and what pretty much all of us would describe as not enough. That's what Jesus holds in His hands this day—*and He looks to His Father and says, "Thanks."*

It isn't a religious motion. It isn't a show for the people. It isn't a formality, like saying grace before supper, or some kind of "trigger" for the miracle to occur. It is, quite simply, Jesus being Jesus. It is a Man—the King of kings and Lord of lords—happy for the little He has.

Yes, Jesus *was* humbleness two thousand years ago. And in the middle of that breathtaking reality He calls to you and me, "Be perfect, therefore, as your heavenly Father is perfect" (Matthew 5:48). In other words, *"Come, be like Me!"*

Humility is such a universally beloved quality in a person. We love to see it in our sports celebrities and public figures. We respect it in our leaders. We say with an admiring smile and approving nod, "He's such a humble person." I can't help but wonder if that's because deep inside, whether we realize it or not, all of us really just want Jesus, and we're naturally drawn to that which bears the fragrance of Him.

Yes, we know humility when we see it: it looks a lot like

Jesus. But how do we "do" humbleness, if I can phrase it that way?

I don't know. Maybe it's a simple matter of caring when you'd rather not, giving when the rules say you have every right to take. Maybe it's taking the time to listen instead of tossing in an opinion. Maybe it's asking the waitress, "How are you this morning?" or giving that coworker who just blew the big deal a break.

Maybe it's saying you're sorry even though you did nothing wrong. Maybe it's spending your Saturday with your aging father, or taking the time to notice the loneliness in your wife's eyes. Maybe it all starts with getting on your face before an awesome God and thanking Him for His goodness toward you, instead of reminding Him about the prayers He hasn't yet answered. I don't know . . .

Several years ago I was in Minnesota at the end of a long day of speaking at a university and doing media interviews. I'd just finished my last interview at a local radio station and had an hour to kill before I went to the airport. The interviewer and I had kind of hit it off, so the two of us stayed there in the sound booth and chatted away.

He was a real family guy and a real blessing of a brother in Jesus. I can't remember all that we talked about, but I asked him about his family, and somewhere in the middle of his answer, he told me a story that took my breath away.

He had come home from work one day, and it had been

"one of those days." It started too early and ended too late; nothing that was supposed to happen happened; everything that could go wrong went wrong; and to top it off, he'd been so busy, he hadn't even stopped to eat. He'd been living on coffee and M&M's the entire day and couldn't wait to sink his teeth into one of his wife's wonderful meals.

As these kinds of days go, this day continued to go. He pulled into his driveway and heard a crunch. It was his son's bicycle lying where it shouldn't have been. Then as he approached the front door, he saw clothing scattered across the garden. The wind had pulled everything off the clothesline, and for some reason his wife hadn't picked them up. So there he was after his horrendous day, picking socks and underwear from between the bushes.

He walked through the door, and the place was a disaster. He had to climb over toys and move the vacuum that was blocking the hallway. The TV was blaring with cartoon madness; one kid was chasing the other and scrambling over the sofa; the smell of diapers in need of changing wafted through the air.

He lifted his nose toward the kitchen, and got what was maybe the worst news of all: he couldn't smell a thing. His wife hadn't even begun cooking. He passed the kids' bedrooms, and the beds weren't made. He turned into the master bedroom, and not even he and his wife's bed was made. And what did he hear coming from the study? His wife was on the phone with her sister who lived up the road, laughing and blabbing away.

It all sounds funny to repeat today, but to this guy at the time, it was anything but funny. He felt the steam rising inside him as his thoughts raced: *What on earth did she do all day? I've been working my tail off, and here she is . . .* You get the idea.

But here's the thing. He didn't react as you or I might expect. Instead, he cleared the dirty clothes from a corner of the bed, plopped himself down, and dropped his head in his hands. He cried a little and began to pray, "Lord, please make me a better husband. Lord, *make me a better husband.*"

Humility—real, true, deep humility—is a breathtaking thing. It's far from easy and it's far from comfortable, but I guess that's because it's so very close to Jesus.

A man sits on the corner of a bed with everything wrong coming at him, and instead of demanding his due, he prays, "Lord, make me a better husband."

And the living God responds, "Yes, My child, I will. I'll make you a better husband; I'll make you a better man. I love you so much, My child. I love you."

JESUS!

A MAN OF PASSION

What kind of desire compels a man to restrain all the power of heaven and earth—all the divinity and dominion of a billion universes—and allow common thugs to slam nails through His hands and feet? What kind of hope? What kind of drive? What kind of excitement and zeal? *What kind of passion*?

It is the most breathtaking act of passionate love in human history—Jesus hanging from a tree. For more than a thousand years He'd wooed and romanced and served His precious "beloved"—His precious people. For more than a thousand years He'd done everything and then some to display His heart, to court His "bride," to draw her back into His arms where she could live safe and secure all her days unto all eternity. Where she could rest and abide in all the goodness that He is and all the treasures He still longs to lavish upon her: "peace . . . which transcends all understanding" (Philippians 4:7); "life . . . to the full" (John 10:10).

I will never leave you nor forsake you.
—Joshua 1:5

I have loved you with an everlasting love.
—Jeremiah 31:3

He provided for her; He parted the Red Sea for her; He made rivers in her deserts; He slew her enemies; He freed her from bondage; He stood between her and her destruction time after time and at turn after turn. "But he brought his people out like a flock; he led them like sheep through the desert. He guided them safely, so they were unafraid; but the sea engulfed their enemies" (Psalm 78:52–53).

He gave her a land to call home. He made her fruitful and endowed her with blessing upon blessing in spite of her weakness and mistakes, regardless of the gash in His heart from her repeated adulteries. Century after century He sent her heroes and kings, deliverers and leaders, prophets and promises, the food of angels, the fire of His glory. When all of that failed to win her affection, He hung on that tree and covered her nakedness with His very own blood. He clothed her shame in His very own glory.

Never has a bride been so desired. Never has a bride been so pursued. Never has a bride been so bejeweled and bedecked— so forgiven, pampered, coddled, and cooed; so cared for, protected, and wept over. Never has a bride been so

breathtakingly,

> passionately,

> > desperately *loved*.

Yes, the story of Jesus—who He was before the beginning, who He was as a Man in the streets of Israel, and who He continues to be today unto eternity—is the most impassioned love story every told. Glory to the Name of Jesus!

Imagine a Man two thousand years ago who walked away from more than all the greatest dreamers and achievers in the world could even begin to dream or build for themselves. There are rulers and world powers, and then there's the King of kings and Lord of lords. There's the amassing of wealth and riches, and then there's "the cattle on a thousand hills" (Psalm 50:10). There are bastions of power and monuments of glory, *and then there's the throne room of the living God.*

Jesus walked away from it all—every position and privilege that divinity affords and every wealth of heavenly dominion. Not even two pennies or a scrap of advantage was held back or reserved. He considered . . . well . . . you and me, and literally "made himself nothing" (Philippians 2:7). He poured Himself out and then continued to pour Himself out, moving through His every day in steadfast purpose and souls-at-stake urgency; giving *all* of His heart, *all* of His mind, *all* of His strength, *all* of His will;

> giving,
>> pursuing,
>>> reaching,
>>>> caring.

JESUS!

There was nothing at all "kick back" about this Man. There was nothing lukewarm or halfway. What the people witnessed in every teaching and every miracle, every touch and every parable, every sparkle in His eye and every glimmer in His smile, was zeal, excitement, pursuit—*passion*. "He put on righteousness as his breastplate, and the helmet of salvation on his head; he put on the garments of vengeance and wrapped himself in zeal as in a cloak" (Isaiah 59:17).

This was not a Man wandering through His life, dropping in on this town and paying a visit to that village, just blessing folks here and blessing folks there. This was not a Man divided between this goal and that desire, this purpose and that comfort, hoping this works out, hoping that comes to be.

This was a Man on a mission—the mission to end all missions. This was a Man who *knew* who He was and what His life was about and wasn't afraid to rise with everything He was, cast His everything into it, and be everything He possibly could be in the middle of it.

To Jesus it didn't matter the cost. It didn't matter the pain—unto death, the pain. With His face set like flint, He pressed on against all odds, against all opposition.

People laughed in His face.

People spit in His face.

People plotted His murder.

But still He pressed on. His blood dripped into the sand, and He pressed on!

Every moment was intentional, birthed in His Father's purpose and timing. Every encounter was in the bull's-eye of His Father's plan. Every move was in perfect accord with His Father's will and His Father's ways.

He was impassioned by His desire for His beloved, His bride—you and me—to see her living in the freedom and fullness she was created to enjoy, to bask eternally in His eternal goodness. "In your majesty ride forth victoriously in behalf of truth, humility and righteousness; let your right hand display awesome deeds. Let your sharp arrows pierce the hearts of the king's enemies" (Psalm 45:4–5).

He was impassioned by His longing to wrap His eternal arms around His beloved's heart—His longing for you and me.

You have stolen my heart, my sister, my bride;
you have stolen my heart with one glance of your eyes,
with one jewel of your necklace.
How delightful is your love, my sister, my bride!
How much more pleasing is your love than wine.
—Song of Songs 4:9–10

Can you imagine the heart that gave birth to those breathtaking verses? Are there words more intimate, more explosive, more, if I may, downright "hot"? Can you imagine the Man who formed those thoughts, the depth of that Man's desire, involvement, and care? *Can you imagine Jesus?*

There He stands in a marketplace of some Galilean hub. He's been moving from town to town, pouring His heart out. He's been sitting with people on street corners and sharing meals with people by campfires, answering all their doubts and confusions, filling them with promise and peace. He's been

working in their fields,
    sleeping on their floors,
        asking for nothing,
            and giving His all.

He's been healing their sick and raising their dead. And with every drop of sweat and every smile, every act of goodness and endurance, He's been reaching over and over to say, "*This is who I am, and you are who I love.*"

JESUS.

For millennia He had contemplated these human days when He would step from all of heaven's glory and into His bride's earthly chamber. Hands-on and eye to eye, He'd bring the Word to life for her—and bring life to her through the Word. With physical fingertips He'd wipe away her physical tears, and with physical voice He'd whisper hope into the private places of her precious soul.

Now here He is, with human feet treading on human ground: Capernaum, Bethsaida, Korazin, Magdala. No village is left out and no villager turned away. He just keeps going and giving.

Take heart, daughter. . . . Your faith has healed you.
—Matthew 9:22

Come, follow me.
—Matthew 4:19

I am willing. . . . Be clean!
—Matthew 8:3

But heartbreak of heartbreaks—by and large the people don't care. The Son of the living God stands before their very eyes. He's the Messiah they've prayed and fasted for, the Anointed One they've dreamed about for generations and placed all their hope in. He's right there in front of them—they can look into His eyes and feel His touch. They can feast on His words and marvel at His wonders. It's so blatantly *Him—but they just don't care.*

Can you imagine Jesus's heart in the middle of such a reality? Put yourself in His shoes. You pay every price there is to pay. You

> love and love,
>> century upon century
>> and now day upon day,

and still they just don't care.

I can only begin to guess at the utter depth of Jesus's heartache as He watches them choose filth and struggle instead of Him. I can only guess at His tears of longing: "If only she would come to Me! None of that other stuff matters—if only she would come to Me!"

Perhaps we can liken it to a dad whose little girl runs away. He only wants the best for her. He only wants to provide and secure—to carry her into the fullness of warmth and goodness and all of the wonder he knows her life can be. Still she goes. She turns her back to him, determined to make her own way.

Oh, the pain of that father—the heartrending pain! He loves her so and *longs* for her return.

A month turns into a year turns into five. He's done

everything he can to woo her back home, and still her room lies empty. Then suddenly one afternoon he sees her. Maybe he's crossing a big-city street on his way to an appointment and happens to look up. And there, through the traffic— there she is!

What would that father do that day? Would he coolly watch her from a distance? Would he look at his watch and say, "I don't want to miss that appointment"? Would he snug up his tie and casually call, "Oh darling! Over here, darling!"

Or would he explode, crying out with everything he had? Can you imagine the surge of excitement that would rocket through that father's heart? Can you imagine how his eyes would grow big and his breath would seize; how he'd run to her through the masses and dart between the cars, caution thrown entirely to the wind? Can you imagine the exultant wail that would volcano from his lungs as he wrapped his arms around her: "My baby, my baby! Please, my baby!"

Two thousand years ago Jesus cried out those oh so familiar words: "Come to me . . . and you will find rest for your souls." (Matthew 11:28–29). I wasn't there and I'm certainly no theologian or scholar, but I have to guess that with so much welling up inside His holy heart, He just couldn't contain Himself for one more second. Oh, how He longs to give the people life. And those words are the key. All they need to do is turn to Him. All they need to do is "Come to me"!

I picture Jesus with tears cascading down His face that day, tears of desperate love—love so desperate that He would soon die for those loved ones. I picture Him on His knees in the dirt with His arms reaching out as far as a man's arms can possibly reach. I picture Him with His heart in His hands and His cry coming from the depths of His being—the eternal, everlasting, generation unto generation, on-every-page-of-your-Bible-and-mine cry of His most yearning heart: "*Come to Me.* I'll give you rest for your souls."

"Please," Jesus weeps in deep, impassioned longing, "I only want to give you rest for your soul."

JESUS.

No, there is nothing lukewarm about this Man. There is nothing halfway, nothing cool, nothing maybe-this or maybe-that. He is a Man who knows who He is and what His life is all about. He knows exactly what He's been born for and exactly what it will cost Him, and He isn't afraid to march headlong into it.

He is impassioned and holy, and His manhood drips from it. He moves with purpose and urgency, never wasting a moment, never moaning about this difficulty or groaning over that frustration. He just moves forward and presses on and presses through.

With the eyes of His heart riveted on souls—oh, precious, precious souls! With His heart pounding in the fullness of kingdom calling. With His Spirit dancing and leaping to the love song of His Father's desire and the beauty of human holiness. With His soul and will, His mind and body, rising to embrace everything of life's adventure, seizing the day like tomorrow will never come.

He stands, Jesus—a Man among men. He stands, Jesus—a Man beyond men. He stands brimming in the largest of His obvious divinity and explosive in the

zeal and passion,
  focus and urgency,
    determination and desire,

blood, sweat, and tears that are cornerstone to His obvious masculinity.

Glory to the Name of Jesus!

It was maybe two years ago that I had the honor of spending an afternoon with a most precious woman who was about seventy years old. I was ministering in a small town in South Africa and was told about her by a pastor.

The film I'd done meant a lot to this woman. She was pretty much confined to a modest nursing home, and loving Jesus like she did, she would sit in her room and watch the movie over and over. "She just sits there and cries tears, she loves Jesus so much," the pastor told me. "And she prays, Bruce. She prays—*for you.*"

As you can imagine, there was no way I was going to leave that town without visiting her, and as I sit here thinking back, I can only praise God that I did. She and I sat together in her little room, and she made me the nicest cup of coffee. Then she told me story after wonderful story.

She told me all about the old days and the way things used to be. She told me how Jesus had carried her through every crisis that life threw at her and then some. She told me how she fell asleep every night dreaming of that moment when He'll hold her in His arms. "We'll waltz across the crystal seas together for all eternity," she said.

She also told me about her husband. He'd passed on a few years earlier, and that's how she ended up in the nursing home. She had two sons, but one was overseas and the other had a busy life with a wife and kiddies of his own. They'd drive out to see her now and again, but to live with them just wasn't practical. So with her husband gone, there was only the nursing home.

But you should have seen her eyes light up when she spoke of him! You should have seen them mist over with tears—tears of love in remembrance and tears of missing him so.

It's a relatively rare man, I think, who leaves his wife cradled in such goodness. It's a rare man who truly makes his wife the "everything" of his eye, the fulfillment of his ambition, the all-consuming desire of his heart. (Is it just me, or did I just describe Jesus?) Yes, there are good men, and yes, there are good marriages, but the kind of relationship I'm talking about—at least from what I can gather—is breathtakingly precious and oh so rare.

This woman enjoyed such a man. The more she spoke of him, the more her eyes sparkled and the more I asked God to make me just like him. He wasn't rich—just a middle-of-the-road guy who worked hard to give her a middle-of-the-road lifestyle. She told me about the day he surprised her with their first new car and how he worked a second job to make the payments on it. She dabbed a tear and giggled as she said, "It was the most awful shade of green, but he was so proud of it." This very blessed guy was her whole life, just as she undoubtedly was his.

But it was one story she shared that brings me to this retelling here. It happened when they were first dating, and for my money it's the most romantic story I've ever heard. (I just wish I were the one who was in it!)

It was summer in the city of Pretoria when they met. They were both a little older. She had been married once before, and back in those days divorce was a scourge and scandal. No man wanted a divorced woman, and every woman whispered behind her back. Even her church treated her "like a leper," she said, so she buried her heart in work and focused on building her own security. She resolved, in fact, to never again marry or have a family. It was difficult to divorce, knowing these were the sacrifices, but the abuse she had endured in

61

her marriage had been too much. Life alone, she decided, was the lesser of two evils.

Then this guy came along. She met him at an open-air fruit market. They started chatting over the mangoes, I guess. He carried her bags home, she made him coffee, and they sat together on her front lawn and laughed for the remainder of the day.

"He never came in the house," she smiled, adding, "Not even to use the 'loo'—and I know he needed to, with all that coffee! He knew the neighbors were watching through their curtains, you see, and he didn't want them to think badly of me."

I don't remember if it was that respect and care that caught her attention, or if it was something else, but the two grew close. "It was difficult to let my guard down," she admitted. "He was so very patient."

Then came the day when she told him of her divorce. "I was thinking I would never see him again, but he got tears in his eyes," she remembered. "It was like his heart broke for me—and he didn't say a word about it. He just had these big tears, and he took my hand and said, 'Will you be my sweetheart?'

"Well, I almost couldn't breathe," she continued. "It was the first time he'd ever taken my hand—and he asked me to be his sweetheart."

That night the two of them had a very special dinner together. He told her to dress nicely, and he took her to a kind of lodge tucked into a local nature reserve. It was one of those places she'd heard about and read about in magazines but only dreamed of ever going to.

He got all dressed up, too, even though he obviously felt awkward in his stiff collar and tie. They were escorted to a candlelit table in the garden, surrounded by nature, beneath the African sky. A vase with white roses (her favorite) was waiting for her. A violinist strolled from table to table.

"It was Valentine's Day," she revealed. "How he found those roses and booked that table he would never, ever tell me. As many times as I asked him through the years, he would just smile and say, 'I love you.'"

Now here is where the story really gets good. That region of South Africa is known for its summer rains. Clouds gather and collide, and out of nowhere comes a deluge. Lightning rips across the sky, and thunder barrels through the hills and valleys. It's all very dramatic and enthralling, all very "Africa."

As fate would have it, the stars that night disappeared and gave way to a warm shower. One by one the couples around them dashed for cover inside the lodge, and in no time they found themselves alone.

There was a canopy umbrella over their table that was just wide enough to shield them if they scooted in tightly. He was not the kind of man to allow a little rain to steal such an evening, so he asked her if she wouldn't mind being a little brave. She didn't want the evening to end either, so they huddled closer together, the rain forming a soft curtain around them, and the magic continued.

But the rain got heavier and heavier. Most everyone else gave up and went home. She said it was extraordinary, though—the quiet, the garden, just the two of them, the rain . . .

The waiter dashed over to check on them. He was a jolly African guy who seemed to enjoy the weather as much as they did. The two men—the waiter and her brand-new sweetheart—had a private chat that she wasn't able to hear. The next thing she knew, the waiter was pulling over umbrellas from all the surrounding tables, creating a more generous cover that would keep them dry, no matter how hard the skies fell.

They sipped their wine. The candles flickered and fluttered in the storm's summer breeze. The violinist joined them beneath the shelter as the rain hid them from the world. Time seemed to stand still.

"And we kissed," she said with a big, *big* smile. "As gently as he'd taken my hand earlier that day, he reached over and cradled my chin. He drew me to him with such care—*as if I were a goddess*—and we kissed and kissed . . ."

Passion—the grasping of life and love and all the wondrous adventure that God intends for life and love to be . . .

A Man of Passion

A man reaches to his wife—his bride—with all that he is. He exalts and treasures her. He covers her with goodness and blankets her with blessing. He counts the "very hairs of [her] head" (Matthew 10:30) and pursues and relishes her. Taking nothing for granted, he approaches every day that God gives them together as if tomorrow may never come, as indeed, it very well may not.

He wakes every morning—a man who knows who he is and what his life is all about. He rises from every challenge that would steal his excitement and beat him down. He stares the enemies of his soul and life's potential straight in the eye and says, "I'm a child of the living God, and you're not going to crush even a moment of the thrill."

He fights off the lukewarm and embraces the red hot. He casts down the pull that would draw him to wander from entertainment to entertainment. And a day becomes a year becomes twenty becomes a lifetime.

Refusing mediocrity, he rolls up his sleeves and dives into each day. He shakes free of fatigue and the aches and pains of life lived in a broken creation, and like an Olympic sprinter in the starting blocks, he digs his heels firmly into every responsibility and purpose God intends for him.

He explodes toward the finish line. He runs "the race" of life in such a way as to "win the prize"—the prize he's already won in Christ Jesus (2 Timothy 4:7; Philippians 3:14).

He worships God. He falls flat on his face and thrusts his hands high in the air. Again, taking nothing for granted, he seeks with all that he is. He cries tears of joy and tears of need and cries out, "Glory, glory!" as he worships his God.

The zeal of the LORD Almighty will accomplish this.
—Isaiah 9:7

Jesus, Jesus, Jesus! Glory to the Name of Jesus!

A MAN OF RESPECT FOR WOMEN

Who a man is in his relationships with women, or in the company of women, reveals so, so much about who that man truly is.

How does a man relate to the women God has placed in his life? How does he approach and regard them? How does he handle and deal with those women, young and old, who have been entrusted to his care or who merely cross his path in the course of daily living? To discover the answers to these questions in terms of a specific man is to discover the man in the middle of them.

A man is blessed by God with a wife. She's not a perfect wife—but then he's not perfect either. How does he treat her in public, when other people are watching? Does he show her respect? Does he treasure her? More importantly, how does he treat her in private, when no one is watching? What goes on behind those closed doors?

Another man is not (at least right now) blessed by God

with a wife. But he sure desires a wife! His eyes are open all day long: "Lord, bless me—today, if possible!" How does he approach the women he meets? What does he say to them, not just with words, but with his undertones and leadings, with the look in his eyes? Is there genuine interest and genuine care, or is he merely seeking his own validation by securing a woman's attention?

Married or otherwise, both men meet and deal with women all through their respective days. They work with women as peers, partners, employers, and employees. They study with women classmates and under women teachers. Women make coffee for them at Starbucks, and they make coffee for women too.

They have mothers and daughters, cousins and aunts. They have nieces and next-door neighbors and the wives and daughters of next-door neighbors. They coach women in softball and work out next to them in the gym. There's Grandma and little sister. There's Great-grandma and *big* sister.

Then there are the women they "meet" on their TV screens and in magazines. The women who smile at them from billboards, computer screens, and CD jackets. The women they see walking through malls or sitting quietly unaware in the cars next to them, waiting for the light to turn green.

How do these men treat these women? What responses rise within them? Are they responses that honor and protect a woman, or are they responses a woman needs protection from?

It's all very challenging and all very true: a man's heart and character are revealed in his actions—and all the more so in his actions *toward women.*

Two thousand years ago Jesus, too, encountered women. He wasn't married or seeking a wife (sorry, *Da Vinci Code*—you lose), but surely, as a very real Man living a very real life, hardly a day went by when He didn't cross paths with a woman.

He worked with women in ministry and healed them through His ministry. He taught them on the hillsides and answered their questions in the marketplaces. He cried tears over their pain and raised their loved ones from the dead. He dealt with them in the ordinary and related to them in the extraordinary. He attended to those women who were entrusted to His care and to so many more whose lives He simply passed along His way.

There was Mary Magdalene; His mother, Mary; and "the other Mary" (Matthew 28:1). There was the mother of Zebedee's sons and the "many women" who followed Him all the way to the cross—women who'd left their homes in Galilee "to care for his needs" (Matthew 27:55).

There was Peter's mother-in-law and the widow who had only two mites. There was precious Talitha, whom He raised from the dead (Mark 5:41), Talitha's mother, and all the women who mourned by her side. There was the woman bleeding from her womb and the woman about to be stoned by the religious elite in the temple courts.

There was the woman from Canaan who had such great faith, and the women of Nazareth who had so little. There was Martha and her sister, yet another Mary. There was the woman whose only son was about to be buried, and the woman who washed His feet in her tears of worship.

Yes, there were many women around Jesus two thousand years ago—and these are only a sampling of those we know about. Through the day-in, day-out of daily life, He undoubtedly met countless more.

He surely laughed and chatted and made friends with women. As a boy, He probably played games with girls in the street; as a Man at the Cana wedding, He possibly enjoyed a dance or two. It was women who accompanied His body to the grave, and it was a woman to whom He first revealed Himself three days later. Glory to the Name of Jesus!

I think of the Samaritan woman drawing water from Jacob's well outside the little town of Sychar. As the story goes, she arrives at the well "about the sixth hour" (John 4:6), in the heat of the day, presumably to be alone. Because of her lifestyle, the other villagers gossip and whisper ugly, damaging words about her. Better to suffer the heat than endure the insults.

This particular day she is met with a surprise, however. There is a Man at the well who is by Himself too—a Man she doesn't recognize. It is the Man Jesus.

Now we don't know much about this Samaritan woman. We can only guess that deep inside, she shares the same "woman realities" that are common to all women. She has dreams and hopes, desires and longings. She has had success in some areas, failure in others. Undoubtedly she has suffered through times of struggle and enjoyed times of great joy. And she has a heart—*a woman's heart*—and all the specifically "woman" sensitivities and strengths that go along with it.

We do know she has made mistakes in her life. Big mistakes. We don't know how old she is, but according to the story, she's had five husbands—and that would have to take a toll on a person, no matter how you cut it. As it is, she is scorned by everyone around her. I can only imagine the up-turned noses she must have received from other women, the filthy flirtations she must have endured from men. No wonder she goes to such lengths to be alone!

But this day she is not alone. What goes through her mind as she looks up and sees Jesus at the well? It's impossible for me or anyone to say. At the same time, considering what was probably her experience of men coming and going, men using her up and then tossing her out, we can speculate: *I wonder what this guy wants. Hmm . . . let me guess.*

Certainly, she is anything but shy before Jesus. In fact, she is downright bold, even saucy. "You are a Jew and I am a Samaritan woman. How can you ask me for a drink?" (John 4:9). Translation: "No Jewish man would even talk to me, but here you are, obviously well out of your way. Cut the game about the water. Why are you *really* here?"

Yes, this is a woman who "knows the score" when it comes to men, and to her human eyes, Jesus would have appeared as ordinary as any other. Little does she know there is nothing ordinary about Him in the least. Little does she know that unlike so many men she's encountered, His ambition is not for her body but for her *eternal soul*.

Now here is where we may get a little uncomfortable, but that's OK. Since it truly is truth, etched unarguably in the Word, and since the Word promises that "the truth will set you free" (John 8:32), I can only trust that its discussion will bring liberation all the more.

By way of groundwork, though, allow me to lay a foundation of absolute honor for Jesus. I *so* love Him, and in what follows, I mean absolutely no irreverence toward Him. I declare before God and man, as loudly as a guy can declare: I am in awe of Jesus. He is the eternal King of Righteousness,

Lord of lords, my God and Savior, who sits at the right hand of the most Holy Father, and I love Him, love Him, *love Him*. Amen and amen!

That said and underscored, let's look at the way Hebrews 4:15 describes Jesus: "For we do not have a high priest who is unable to sympathize with our weaknesses, but we have one who has been tempted *in every way, just as we are*—yet was without sin." Hebrews 2:17 makes the same point: "For this reason he had to be made *like his brothers in every way*, in order that he might become a merciful and faithful high priest."

Now, wait a minute. Did the Holy Spirit, through the writer of Hebrews, just say that Jesus was tempted *just as you and I are?* Did He say "in every way"? Does that mean (gulp) even *that* way?

My goodness—*He knows*. As a Man two thousand years ago, He walked the same roads and stood at the same crossroads familiar to us all. He understands the struggles and weaknesses of the human heart and human flesh. Though completely victorious, He wrestled with the exact same temptations we do. Glory to the Name of Jesus!

So there He is, sitting by a well, being approached by an "experienced" woman with presumption dangling from her eyes.

Did Jesus find Himself in the middle of Hebrews 4:15

that day? I don't know—no one can know. I do know He was tired, hungry, far from home, and all alone (John 4:6–8). I know He is able to sympathize with my weaknesses today because, two thousand years ago, as the Scriptures so clearly say, He experienced them too.

I also know that Jesus, at thirty years young, was every bit a Man in every manly way, if I may phrase it that way. Forgive me, but there can be no doubt that He would have humanly desired the holy treasures of female companionship within the holiness of marriage, as would any man. He would have experienced longing for those sacred intimacies and loneliness for lack of them.

In fact, I'm going to guess Jesus would have experienced those desires and longings even more. Given the perfection of His understanding and His divine awareness of how truly wondrous married companionship is intended to be, I can't even begin to imagine the depth of His human loneliness. In fact, may I toss something out there, as food for thought? *Jesus was the loneliest Man who ever was.*

JESUS!

No one knows whether Jesus tasted weakness at that Samaritan well. What we do know (and this is *so* exciting) is that even if He did, something greater than weakness rose inside Him and drove Him victoriously past it.

This was a Man who knew who He was and what His life was all about. He knew who His Father was and what His Father was all about. He knew the works His Father called Him to do and the Man His Father called Him to be.

This was a Man whose eyes were so remarkably riveted on the plans and purposes His Father set before Him that literally *nothing* could get in the way. There was no struggle bigger; the pain—no matter. There was only His commitment to His Father and His commitment to you and me, and these were so much greater than any human weakness that might have invited Him to respond in a humanly weak way.

There was also His commitment to that woman. Jesus *knew* that woman—His understanding was divine. He knew her name. He knew every hair on her head. He knew all the mistakes she had made and every tear she had shed because of them. He knew every hope His Father had for her and everything of goodness His Father wanted her life to be.

He cared for her. He deeply, genuinely cared. If there was weakness that day, well, there was weakness. But far—*so far*—beyond that, crushing that, washing it over with living waterfalls of godly, pure, life-giving love, He knew this was a precious woman who was oh so broken, and He cared.

He knew something else too. It's something that a lot of us men know in our heads about the women around us but so often don't show in our actions. Despite her mistakes, Jesus knew who this woman *truly* was in the eyes of His Father and in the cradle of His Father's heart: *a daughter of the Most High King!*

Yes, El Shaddai, the Wonder and Glory, the Master and Most Eminent Majesty of all Creation, looked upon this Samaritan woman—this ever-so-precious woman—and saw His own daughter. Just as He does when He looks upon your wife, your mother, your sweetheart, your grandma, the girl who serves you at McDonalds, the little old lady who sits next to you in church. The woman at the well was the princess of the King of Glory. She was *the living God's little girl*.

So Jesus moves in absolute tenderness, respect, and care. He stops everything He is doing and takes the time. "If you knew the gift of God and who it is that asks you for a drink, you would have asked him and he would have given you living water" (John 4:10).

He honors her with grace and kindness,
    treasures her with gentleness,
        and nurtures her with understanding.

"Whoever drinks the water I give him will never thirst" (v. 14).

He doesn't just talk; He listens to her heart. "What you have just said is quite true" (v. 18). When He speaks, He speaks from *His* heart. "Indeed, the water I give him will become in him a spring of water welling up to eternal life" (v. 14).

He builds a wall of truth around her; He protects her with leadership. "Believe me, woman, a time is coming . . . and has now come" (vv. 21–23). He covers her with value and dignity. "I who speak to you am he" (v. 26).

He coddles and uplifts where others have abused and torn down. He gives where others have taken. He chooses to be the healer of her wounds, where other men have chosen to add to them. He fosters her purpose (the entire town is saved through her), where others have pursued their own. He woos her into the arms of her loving heavenly Father, where others have only seduced her unto themselves.

And therein is the bottom line, really. Therein is "the Jesus difference." Therein is the fountainhead out of which flows everything of His character and everything of His manhood, most especially in relationship to women: He is completely, utterly selfless before her.

JESUS.

His purpose is

her well-being,
> *her* goodness,
>> *her* fruitfulness.

His heart is entirely for her, and He gives Himself entirely to her. There is no consideration of His own needs—there never was with Jesus. There is no, "What can I gain from this woman?" He is all about *her*.

There is only joy in His heart toward her and humility in His posture before her. There is only desire to breathe new life into every corner of her being, to bless her, to uphold her, to be the one Man who honors and protects her, who restores her dignity and sets her free to be everything her "Daddy" birthed her to be. Glory to the Name of Jesus!

What would it have been like to be that woman—or any woman—meeting Jesus two thousand years ago? What would a woman have seen in His eyes, heard in His tone, felt in His touch?

Strength,

gentleness,

warmth,

genuineness.

A woman meeting Jesus would have met a Man who was confident enough to be tender, secure enough to openly care. She would have met a Man who led in graciousness and humility, whose touch on her shoulder was giving and pure.

And what message would she have sensed in His manner? What would His every move have whispered into her heart? What would she have felt about herself after being with Him?

"You, oh precious one, are My Daddy's most precious daughter—a true princess—a daughter of the Most High King!"

Jesus, Jesus, Jesus! Glory to the Name of Jesus!

For a long time now, I have been running around the globe sharing Jesus with folks through a speaking ministry. I've been in so many varied and sundry venues and surroundings, it would make my head spin to recount them all. I've spoken in everything from soup kitchens to football stadiums, from corporate lunchrooms to some of America's most respected churches. But over all those years and through all those events, I don't know if there's one I treasure in my heart more than the afternoon I spent ministering to a gathering of women who (buckle your seat belt) "worked" in a brothel.

I'll never forget the invitation, which, as you can imagine, came as quite a shock. I'd spoken to a youth group in this particular community the night before and got a call from the youth pastor's assistant, Tony. Tony was a Bible student—one of those guys with the joy of knowing Jesus splashed all over his face all the time. Young and newly married, he was so excited to be serving, so aware of God's grace—so truly in awe of it all.

"Bruce, this is a little different," Tony admitted on the phone that morning, "but how would you like to minister to the girls in a brothel?" He told me that he ministered to them regularly—in fact, he held a service for them every Sunday. Interestingly enough, they loved the film I did in which I played Jesus. He said they had it among the videos on their shelf and watched it often. When they heard I was in town, they asked him if he could arrange for me to come by.

How could I say no to an invitation like that? Call it a sense of adventure or an awareness that this was where the ministry rubber hit the ministry road; I don't know. It felt as if the Lord was challenging me to put my ministry money where my ministry mouth was, if you know what I mean.

It's easy to stand on the platform of a church on a Sunday morning or chat with Terry Meeuwsen on *The 700 Club*, but to sit in a brothel on a Wednesday afternoon—that's a whole other thing. So the next day there I was, ringing a doorbell in a middle-class neighborhood and sitting in a living room surrounded by these girls—these

rejected,
used,
pained,
broken girls.

It was an incredible experience, to say the least. It was absolutely breathtaking to experience God's goodness in a place like that and see His grace flow so openly. But all that is another story for another time. The reason I bring it up is to tell you about Tony.

As the madam in the brothel explained, earlier that year one of her girls had been killed in an automobile accident.

The girl had no family that anyone knew of. The madam and the other girls were her only real family. They were the ones to whom her body was released. They were the ones who would have to plan her funeral and pay for her burial.

So they began to make arrangements. A date was picked, and the body was taken to a funeral home. The girls pooled their money and bought a new dress for the girl to be buried in. They purchased a casket and a plot of soil. Everything was ready. The only thing missing was a pastor, a preacher, a "man of God" to perform a service or at least say a few words at the graveside.

Needless to say, these were not women who went to church. It wasn't that they didn't want to; it was that they were too ashamed and afraid. They also knew they would run into some of their customers there—but that's another story for another time too.

Anyway, since they had no church home or pastoral connection, the madam simply opened the Yellow Pages and began phoning. "I'm so-and-so," she'd say. "One of our girls has died, and we need someone to come and do a funeral service."

She called almost every church in the area, and across the board she was turned down. She had the phone slammed in her ear a couple of times; she was scolded and even called names. She told me the prevailing response was, "We don't deal with your kind."

Now maybe she was exaggerating a bit. Maybe half of what she said was truth and half of it was hurt; I don't know. All I know is that no one would come out to do a service for this poor girl or at least say a few words at the cemetery—no one, that is, except Tony.

The madam told me she got a call from him one day. They didn't know each other, but the way I understand it, Tony had heard about the situation from a friend who was a social worker. He phoned the madam and said, "I'm not a pastor or anything. I'm just a Bible student. But I'd be happy to come out, if you'd like me to." With no other option, the madam said yes, and the next morning Tony found himself in the living room of the brothel and then at the graveside, sharing the love of Jesus with twenty or so of these—yes—precious daughters of the Most High King.

As Tony told me his side of the story, he just giggled. All he could talk about was how faithful God was. He asked the madam if he could come to the home every Sunday and "have church" with the girls. He'd bring a friend with a guitar, and they'd sing a little bit. He'd bring the girls Bibles and preach the Word. He'd pray for them and lay their needs before God.

By the time I got there that Wednesday afternoon, Tony had developed quite a strong relationship with these girls. You should have seen the way the whole place lit up when he walked in the door. The most hardened faces broke into smiles when he hugged them. Some eyes even welled with tears.

He'd been faithfully serving them Sunday after Sunday, often stopping by during the week when he was in the neighborhood. They trusted Tony—they knew he genuinely, truly cared. He didn't judge them, tell them how to live their lives, or come as one who was spiritually superior.

He didn't even try to set their lives straight—He knew God was big enough to take care of that in His time and His way. *He just handled them with respect and value.* He chatted with them eye to eye. He didn't make jokes about their "profession" or scowl at them when they were obviously drunk or high.

He just served them. He was the one guy who was *faithful* to them. He treated them with

tenderness,

righteousness,

warmth,

and goodness.

He gave them back their dignity and led them into the safety of their heavenly Father's arms—into the holy embrace of the Man Jesus, living and breathing in a Bible student named Tony.

That brothel is closed down now. It doesn't exist anymore. Just last year I was in that same city and ran into that social worker—that friend of Tony's who'd first told him about the place. It seems that one by one the girls all came around. They got born again. They rose in their understanding of who they truly were in Jesus. They rose in the strength His grace provides. They rose in the hope of their salvation and the "nothing is impossible" that God had for their lives.

They rose so much that they all quit the brothel, got real jobs, and settled into legitimate lifestyles. The social worker told me that two or three of them even enrolled in Bible school. Who knows, maybe Tony is one of their teachers.

A man treats a woman with respect. He cares. He offers her dignity and gentleness. He gives when the tide says "take." He builds safety around her. He

> nurtures,
>
> > encourages,
> >
> > > honors,
> > >
> > > > and leads.

He values her as the living God's precious, precious daughter. He values her as she truly is.

As that woman looks into such a man's eyes, in her heart she hears a most holy whisper: *"Jesus, Jesus, Jesus."*

Glory to the Name of Jesus!

A Man of Grace in Speech

Grace. It is the all-encompassing, five-letter summation of the Son of the living God.

Two thousand years ago, as Jesus stood as a Man, the word literally defined Him, just as He defined it. Two thousand years ago, Jesus didn't merely extend grace or even author grace—He literally *was* grace. He was its personification, its human reality, its manifest consciousness.

"The Word became flesh" (John 1:14), and grace *was* the Word. It was the essence of Jesus's being,

the declaration of His Person,
the perfection of His purpose,
the excellence of His manhood.

Living, breathing *grace*.

JESUS!

The truth of grace can be a challenge, though. Indeed, it is probably the greatest challenge in all of Christendom.

Over the centuries, has there been any reality more contradicted and defaced, more painted over with rules and proclamations of "Yeah, but . . ."? Has there been any reality more doctrinally bantered, more scholarly beaten up, more—oh so tragically—tossed aside entirely?

Grace is also an unwitting victim to that old adage "Familiarity breeds contempt." It is no less vital than breathing and so unfathomably deep, yet like a diamond dropped in the sand, it so readily disappears into the basket of Christian clichés. It becomes little more than "today's devotional," a study lesson, a doctrinal tenet, a rote religious term.

Hopefully I'm wrong, but I would guess that if you were to poll a thousand non-Christians, asking them what they thought Christianity was, not one of them would say, "God's grace." They may say, "Conservative values." They may say, "Following the Bible." They may even come close with something like, "Believing the teachings of Jesus." But I would be hard pressed to think that even one would smile and say, "God's grace."

Two thousand years ago, in the company of Jesus, that would not have been the case. Grace literally gushed from His being. It poured from His presence in rivers of

> mercy and kindness,
> > patience and gentleness,
> > > self-control and forgiveness.

To look into His eyes was to be overwhelmed with humility and encouragement, self-sacrifice and faithfulness, approachability and compassion, leadership and truth. He was always giving—*to the point of being nailed to a tree.*

All day long, every single day, Jesus moved in grace and walked in grace. He acted and reacted entirely in grace. It was the most comprehensive, underlying, over-blanketing constant that spilled from His every miracle and His every teaching, His every drop of sweat and every drop of blood. Even His Name, *Jesus*—"God saves"—meant grace.

JESUS.

Can you imagine being one of Jesus's apostles, or Mary Magdalene, or anyone else who enjoyed the greatest honor ever bestowed in all of human history: living face to face, day to day, eye to eye, and hands-on with the Son of the living God?

That which was from the beginning, which we have heard,
which we have seen with our eyes, which we have
looked at and our hands have touched—
this we proclaim concerning the Word of life.
—1 John 1:1

Wow, wow, triplewow! Does the thought of it not fill you with awe? John was able to pen those words because he saw Jesus with his own eyes. He slept next to Him and ate meals with Him. He actually *touched* Him—the Son of the living God!

He witnessed the heartbreak in His tears and the kingdom joy in His laughter. He sat in the temple courtyards with Him and on the hillsides and street corners, wrapping his being around it all.

He saw every eyeful and heard every earful. He sat by campfires with Him, walked side by side for hours and just talked and talked with Him—the Son of the living God!

Oh, wonder of wonders! Can you even begin to imagine what that would be like, to actually hear Him speak—to drink of the living water that cascaded from His words? To be led by those words along "paths of righteousness" unto "green pastures" and "quiet waters" (Psalm 23:1–3)? To taste their sweet manna of hope, care, goodness, and glory in the

deepest,

most guarded,

and most hungry places of your heart?

All spoke well of him and were amazed at the gracious words that came from his lips.
—Luke 4:22

Words, words—the power of words! And, though less regarded, the power (maybe even greater power) of the way in which words are spoken!

Words can kill—and how tragically many of us know that. "What's wrong with you?" "You'll never amount to anything." "I wish you were never born!" Oh, the lives upon lives that have been shipwrecked, that have never come close to their fullest potential, because of such reckless, death-dealing words.

Words can also give life. "I'm so proud of you." "You're an awesome kid." "Yeah, give it a try. You can do it." "I love you so much." What a treasure to have one's soul so nurtured, to live so validated, so encouraged and upheld. To have such life breathed into one's being, breeding

> hope and goodness,
> calm and contentment,
> ease and achievement,
> value and maturity.

The tongue has the power of life and death,
and those who love it will eat its fruit.
—Proverbs 18:21

A man finds joy in giving an apt reply—
and how good is a timely word!
—Proverbs 15:23

Out of the overflow of the heart the mouth speaks. The
good man brings good things out of the good stored up in him.
—Matthew 12:34–35

But I tell you that men will have to give account on the day of judgment for every careless word they have spoken.
—Matthew 12:36

Reckless words pierce like a sword,
but the tongue of the wise brings healing.
—Proverbs 12:18

Again I say, the power of words!

And so much more, the power of words *spoken by Jesus*!

Let's listen to His words—no, *feel* His words—just as someone would have felt them two thousand years ago. Let's pretend they're not Scripture for just a moment. Let's set aside all the leather-bound pomp and posture and listen to them *with our hearts . . .*

He turns—He smiles. His face is warm and genuine, rugged and tan. Perspiration glistens lightly on His forehead. He reaches a strong, calloused hand to cradle your shoulder. His grip is calm, selfless, and sure.

He looks into your eyes. His lips begin to move. He speaks. He's the Son of the living God, and He speaks:

"Peace I leave with you. My peace, I give to you."

"Before Abraham was born, I am."

"Come . . . you will find rest for your soul."

"I no longer call you servant—I call you friend."

"Don't be afraid; only believe."

"I am willing; be clean."

"Your sins have been forgiven."

"I am the living bread that came out of heaven."

"I am the good shepherd."

"As My Father loved Me, so I have loved you."

"Remain in My love."

". . . rest for your soul . . ."

Can you hear the support and encouragement, the love beating in the holiness of His heart? Every word gives; every word treasures. Every word

coddles and cares,
    leads and inspires,
        calms and assures,
            blesses and uplifts.

Every word is that "tree of life" under whose shade alone is rest for the tired heart, freedom for the shackled spirit, repair for the broken soul.

Every word breathes the same wonder over and over: "I love you. I'm the Son of the living God, and I love you." Oh, grace upon living grace! Praise the Name of Jesus!

And therein is the key. Therein is that golden reality that underscored His every "Be healed" and His every "Woe to you!" two thousand years ago. It permeated His every phrase and impregnated His every pause. It exploded from His harshest rebukes and whispered from His most intimate summons. It was as alive and apparent when Jesus belted, "You hypocrites!" as it was when He hugged the kiddies and giggled, "For the kingdom of God belongs to such as these" (Mark 10:14).

It was beneath His every line and between His every word, cascading from His lips like streams of living water, resonating the unceasing cry of His holy heart, over and over without bias or reserve: "I love you. I'm *for* you.

If you're thirsty, come.

If you're broken, come.

If you despise Me, come.

I love you. Come!"

Yes, our "Father in heaven is not willing that any . . . should be lost" (Matthew 18:14), so there wasn't one soul Jesus approached in any other way. A stone-wielding Pharisee, a woman bleeding from her womb, a rich young ruler, a man blind from birth, a Roman soldier with a hammer and three nails—there wasn't one to whom He spoke with any less desire or hope than any other; not one He addressed with any less passion, promise, heart, or healing.

"You snakes! You brood of vipers!" (Matthew 23:33). *I love you, I love you.*

"You of little faith, . . . why did you doubt?" (Matthew 14:31). *I love you, I love you.*

"How long shall I stay with you? How long shall I put up

with you?" (Matthew 17:17). *I love you, I love you, I love you.*

"For God did not send his Son into the world to condemn the world, but to save the world through him" (John 3:17). Jesus was

> *always* reaching out,
>> *always* extending grace,
>>> *never* pushing away,
>>>> *never* writing *anyone* off.

Maybe there were tears streaming down His face as He spoke some of those seemingly hard statements. Maybe He was kneeling on the pavement, pleading with outstretched arms. Maybe He was clutching that epileptic's father in an impassioned embrace as He whispered, "O unbelieving and perverse generation," from a depth of heartbrokenness that you and I will never know (Matthew 17:17).

Maybe there was a smile stretched across His face, or maybe He tossed laughter into the air and an arm around Peter's shoulder when He asked, "Are you still so dull?" (Matthew 15:16).

Maybe. No one knows one way or the other. But we do know what the Word of God unequivocally says, and we can trust that it's true: *His lips were anointed with grace.*

Strongly belted or tenderly whispered, every word was the "balm in Gilead" (Jeremiah 8:22) for the wounded soul. Every syllable was a life raft for the overwhelmed, a fortress for the tormented and scared. Every phrase was a refuge for the weak and weary, a road map for the confused and lost. Every sentence was an embrace for the forgotten and rejected, a most holy salvation for the sinfully enslaved.

Two thousand years ago, in the streets and alleyways of ancient Israel, there was not one man or woman, granny or child, who didn't walk away from Jesus knowing in their heart of hearts, *this Man loves me. this Man deeply cares.*

It's true that many spurned that care. Twisted in their understanding by a cunning spiritual adversary, mistaking His grace for something to fear, many—heartbreakingly—walked away. But for a few moments at least, before their minds and hearts were darkened, His words left no doubt: *This Jesus truly cares.*

What a challenge Jesus's example sets! Especially for those of us who are men, it is one of the greatest challenges of our lives: that through our speech and by the fruit of our lips, we would wrap those whom God has entrusted to our care in the same kind of unquestionable security. That whether we're applying discipline or just conversing on the way home from school, our kids would never have reason to doubt "my Dad loves me." That whether we're working through conflict or enjoying a candlelight dinner, our wives or girlfriends would always know "this man truly cares" and never have cause to question or fear.

Yes, it's a huge Jesus-challenge, guys: that a man would so guard his mouth that no careless words would ever be spoken, and no words would be spoken in a careless way. That no matter the circumstances or the pull of self-interest, a man would choose to speak with "Jesus lips"—lips anointed with grace.

Never once did a coarse joke or snide chuckle leak from Jesus's mouth two thousand years ago. Never once did He slip into a disrespectful flirtation or go off on a "know-it-all" challenge. Never once did Jesus use words to put down, gain advantage, take, manipulate, or control. Rather, He *blessed*. Glory to the Name of Jesus!

It would only be a short season before the same people who tasted His care in the streets and synagogues of Galilee and Judea would see Him hanging on a tree outside Jerusalem. It's not that they would have recognized Him: "His appearance was so disfigured beyond that of any man and his form marred beyond human likeness" (Isaiah 52:14). It's that they would have heard "the buzz" all through the city: "They're crucifying Jesus!" They would have run to Golgotha to see with their own eyes. And as they looked up, they would have read the words, "The King of the Jews," dangling so ironically above His head.

What any of them may have been thinking that day, no one knows. But standing there, perhaps remembering back to a miracle Jesus did, or a kindness He showed, or a lesson He taught, they would have witnessed a *most* remarkable scene . . .

Jesus is only moments from death. There's blood, well, everywhere. Suddenly, in a feat of extraordinary will, struggling against extraordinary pain, He lifts His head. He forces open an eye. He looks toward a woman everyone knows is His mother, a man everyone knows is His friend.

The two draw close—close enough to hear. His lips quiver—lips that had always been anointed with grace, but now lie torn and shredded because of it. Through the blood that bubbles from between them, He speaks.

"Dear woman," Jesus whispers, "Here is your son." His head tips toward His friend. "Here is your mother." (John 19:26–27). Moments later, He is no more.

"Mom, I'm going where you can't follow right now, but John will take care of you, OK? I trust him. You can trust him too. I love you, Mom."

"John, you've been so faithful. I love you so much. Please take care of My mama for me. I'm putting her in your hands. Take good, good care of her. Thanks."

JESUS.

His lips were anointed with grace, even in the darkest and most terrible moments of His ultimate display of grace. Just as salvation ran red and dripped from His toes into the sand beneath His feet, care and tenderness fell from His lips into the pain of His mother's heart and the needs of her life situation. Even on that day—that day and every day—the words were as true as His Word is always true: "You are the most excellent of men, and your lips are anointed with grace."

JESUS!

I'm going to sound like a pretty typical uncle right now, but my nephews and my niece are *very* special kids. They have an absolute ball in their three little lives. Fun and more fun is the order of the day, and I'm talking about *good* fun.

If it's not raining, they're scooted outdoors. "Go outside and play. Build something, dig tunnels, play ball, go for a swim." My brother and sister-in-law have created an environment for their kids that strongly cultivates creativity, exploration, and hands-on "doing," as opposed to sitting in their rooms with headphones on or disappearing into video games. The blessing that has flowed as a result is clear: the kids are thriving in every way. Glory to Jesus!

Nicholas is the oldest. He's going to be the next "Crocodile Hunter"—he just *loves* creatures, especially reptiles. He knows everything there is to know about them and handles them with fearlessness, respect, and ease.

Nicholas's sport is golf, and his other interests range from NASCAR to art to the Los Angeles Angels. He's fifteen years old at the time of this writing, and he goes to community college: I rest my case.

Next there's Dean, who is following in his uncle's footsteps as an actor. Dean goes out on a lot more auditions than I do (not that I've noticed), and it's not just a pipe dream—the kid is good. He did his first film with Tony Danza, and Tony was astounded by his abilities.

Dean's got a bit of a conflict, though. His dramatic talent is exceeded only by his baseball prowess. I was watching one of his games just last week. He came up to bat, and on the first pitch, *crash!* Over the center-field fence. Go Dean!

Then there's my niece, Melinda, who's the whole reason I'm telling this story. What can I say about Melinda, except that she has my heart securely tucked into her back pocket.

Melinda is a little ballet dancer and a bit of an actor too. She was on stage in *Fiddler on the Roof* a while back when one of the adult professional actors forgot her lines. All the actors froze—except Melinda. She just smiled, piped up with an ad lib that fit right into the scene, and got the whole cast back on track. She was all of eight years old at the time. Welcome to Melinda!

Melinda plays quite a game of basketball; she's the star of her girls' league team. She's also got a rather extensive collection of stuffed animals that not only perform in a variety of living-room shows, but are very enterprising as well. They've had living-room restaurants, hardware stores, and even a gourmet coffee shop. Every business venture they've pursued has turned an extraordinary profit. Who needs Warren Buffett when you've got Antonio, the stuffed gorilla?

I could tell many Melinda stories, but the one I think portrays her best took place at Disneyland when she was about seven. My brother took her into Mickey Mouse's "film studio" (you know, over there in Toontown) to meet the Mouse guy himself. There was Mickey, live and in person, and little Melinda trotted right up to him.

As my brother describes it, the two were hugging, and out of nowhere Melinda reached up and tweaked Mickey's nose. As you can imagine, Mickey was kind of shocked (being a star of his stature and all), and he rubbed his nose as if it were sore. With the precious moment somewhat spoiled, Melinda moved on, and Mickey turned his attention elsewhere.

Once they got outside the studio, my brother stooped down and asked Melinda, "Why did you tweak Mickey on the nose like that?" Melinda looked him in the eye—"as if I were the dumbest guy on the planet," he says—and declared, "*His nose is plastic!*" Again, welcome to Melinda!

Just last week I was up at my brother's house having dinner after a sun-drenched day of backyard baseball and all sorts of great fun. It's always the custom for Melinda to sit next to Uncle Bruce at dinner (or maybe I should say, for Uncle Bruce to sit next to Melinda). Then, between dinner and desert, Melinda climbs into her uncle's lap, and there she stays till the party is over.

I must tell you, when little Melinda sits in my lap like that, and we're just laughing and enjoying, it's like I've died and gone to heaven. Truly, I could just stay there for all eternity. It's like, "You can take me right now, Lord, because life just doesn't get any better."

Well, we were sitting there eating out of each other's ice cream bowls that night, and as I looked at her, I was just so "taken." She's so precious, such a little treasure, so happy and winsome and engaging! She was chatting up a storm, making little jokes, and giggling with glee. At one point I just couldn't help myself. Smiling from ear to ear, I caught her eye and said, "Do you know how beautiful you are, Melinda?"

Melinda never broke my gaze. She didn't answer at first. It was as if she was thinking about my question. It was as if she wanted to answer truthfully and so was taking her time, repeating the question silently to herself. Then, as matter-of-fact, as innocent and humble, as unaffected and vulnerable as can be, she just smiled a tiny, pensive smile and said, "*Yeah*."

Mine was a question that wasn't really a question. It was my way of telling her something. But little Melinda didn't need Uncle Bruce to tell her how beautiful a person she is. *She already knew.*

Raised in an environment of goodness and care, led by lips that bless and assure, parented with encouragement and nurture, her little being bathed in "I love you" and "You can do it"—beautiful Melinda already knew.

There isn't a day that goes by in her wondrous little world that Melinda isn't told how precious she is. There isn't a day that she doesn't know she's treasured. She doesn't wrestle with rejection or low esteem, as many little girls do. She doesn't look at the TV and think, *I wish I were like her.* There's no overcompensating in behavior or following-the-crowd in dress. She's entirely content and entirely secure; so creative, inquisitive, happy, and sure. Her little soul—her heart and the imaginings of her mind—is healthy and whole.

How does that which is so very rare happen for a little girl? I don't know; I've never had kids of my own, and I'm certainly no expert on child rearing. But I do know that Melinda's dad and mom endlessly and unceasingly validate and support her. I can tell you I've never once heard a death-dealing phrase in that house—never a "Why are you so stupid?" "What's wrong with you?" "Don't waste your time; you'll never make it."

Never once have those kids been criticized for trying something that didn't work out. Never once have they been discouraged from exploring something new. They're always upheld, encouraged, guided, then released to explore and be-come everything God intends them to be.

My brother and his wife breathe a constant stream of life, love, and security into their children's lives. They breathe en-couragement and support into their children's dreams. And with every breath, they breed

hope and calm,
contentment and ease,
achievement, value, and maturity.

It was a two-and-a-half-hour drive home for me that night. I remember I left very late, because it was so difficult to pull myself away. There was hardly another car on the highway as I wound through the California hills and glided along the California seacoast. I had the windows rolled down and the heater blasting, as is my custom on those long, star-sparkled, solo night drives. I didn't turn the radio on once, though. I didn't plug in one CD. I just couldn't stop thinking about that moment, "*Yeah*," and precious little Melinda who already knew.

A man speaks into his child's life with lips of grace; a mother nurtures with words that empower and secure. That child grows up and lives her life in the fullness of all God has for her, born in the wonder of what she "already knows."

For out of the overflow of his heart
his mouth speaks.
~Luke 6:45

The tongue that brings healing is a tree of life.
~Proverbs 15:4

You are the most excellent of men and
your lips have been anointed with grace.
~Psalm 45:2

JESUS!

A Man of Fearlessness before Men

There are men who fear God . . . and there are men who fear men.

That's a very black-and-white statement, I know, and it may not be entirely fair. After all, no one is perfect. There's undoubtedly a flip-flopping between the two that all of us engage in to one degree or another. We're born with a sin nature, and as hard as we may try, this side of heaven, none of us will ever be 100 percent "there."

There is another reason we flip-flop as we do. Fear of God is a direct outflow of knowing who God is. To know Him is to fear Him in the most healthy and holy of ways. The degree to which a man knows God is the degree to which he fears Him.

But here's a Catch-22—one that actually lets us all breathe a little easier: "Oh, the depth of the riches of the wisdom and knowledge of God! How unsearchable his judgments, and his paths beyond tracing out!" (Romans 11:33). In other words, the most knowledgeable among us can't even come close to fully knowing Him. That's how big and beyond comprehension God is.

Still, men have caught glimpses of Him through the ages, unedited and unfogged by the limits of human interpretation. Interestingly enough, every one of those men had the exact same reaction: *They crumbled before Him in awe and trembling*. They were consumed in fear of Him. Everything of their lives suddenly meant nothing. There was just Him!

"Woe to me!" the prophet Isaiah cried when he saw God in a vision. "I am ruined! For I am a man of unclean lips, and I live among a people of unclean lips, and my eyes have seen the King, the LORD Almighty" (Isaiah 6:5). One face-to-face glimpse, and Isaiah was reduced to weeping and wailing for the sin in his life and the lives of all those around him.

Daniel didn't fare much better: "As he came near the place where I was standing, I was terrified and fell prostrate" (Daniel 8:17). "I had no strength left, my face turned deathly pale and I was helpless" (Daniel 10:8).

When Ezekiel saw God he "fell facedown" (Ezekiel 1:28) and was immobilized for a week. "I came to the exiles who lived at Tel Abib near the Kebar River," he said. "And there, where they were living, I sat among them for seven days—*overwhelmed*" (Ezekiel 3:15).

Then there's Moses, who is arguably the greatest leader in all of human history. He was the deliverer of the Israelite nation, handpicked and appointed by God Himself. He sat at God's feet for weeks upon weeks atop Mount Sinai. He was the trustee of God's covenant, the parter of the Red Sea.

Moses cried out, "Now show me your glory" (Exodus 33:18), and God actually did it. Afterward the reflected glory shone so brightly on Moses's face that he wore a veil in the presence of the people (Exodus 34:33–35).

One would think that after that, Moses would be pretty excited about himself, if I may phrase it that way. He certainly had every right to be.

But the truth is so shockingly the opposite. Numbers 12:3 records one of the most breathtaking, mind-bending, and personally challenging realities in all of Scripture: "Now Moses was a very humble man, more humble than anyone else on the face of the earth."

My goodness! Is that what happens to a man when he *really* knows God? Quaking in awe, trembling in fear, he becomes "more humble than anyone else on the face of the earth"? Glory to the Name of Jesus!

Then there's fear of men—men giving men what only God deserves.

A man stands between honoring God in a situation or advancing his own cause. Heartbreak of heartbreaks, he bows to the latter. He chooses scriptures that (seem to) support him. He interprets the more troubling ones away.

He grovels before "everyone is doing it." "If you want to get ahead" sits firmly on his throne. He grins and admires ungodly men because of their position and power. He applauds their systems and seeks their favor. After all, "Look what it will mean for me! God wants to bless me, and I just have to clear the way."

Yes, the throne of a man's heart and life is often occupied by so many other things: dollar-envy, career success, the desires of his heart. "The guys might not like me." "She might not like me." "Don't upset the apple cart." "I don't want to be alone."

Want, ambition, fear of consequence—they grip a man's devotion, and oh so sadly he "sells" his God and his manhood away.

Two thousand years ago in the streets and marketplaces of ancient Israel, Jesus had absolutely *no* fear of man. In singular and unwavering devotion, He was nothing less than a champion for His Father, a Man beyond men, and all that His Father meant for a man to be.

Can you imagine Jesus that day in the temple courts, with all those moneychanger tables and hawker booths lying in ruins about Him (John 2:13–16)? Can you imagine that whip of cords twisted in His calloused grip, the fire in His eyes, the set of His jaw, the sweat dripping from His tanned and taut brow?

A scramble of "lesser men" scurry and crawl around His feet, scratching and clawing for the pennies and pittance that lie scattered on the pavement. Like a mountain of manliness, Jesus stands solitary among them—*the living, breathing Son of the living God.*

What a picture of righteousness!

What a picture of glory!

What a picture of what God intends every man to be!

If I may, Jesus was no dummy that day. He knew He was signing His death warrant when He exploded as He did. He was perfectly aware that the religious elite—the guys with the money, power, and position, who so many others tiptoed around and played up to—would respond by meeting in secret to plot His end.

Jesus knew all that and then some. *But He did it anyway!* Oh, the heroism of the Man; the bravery, nobility, dignity, and courage. Oh, the sureness of self and the single-mindedness before God!

Whether it was that day or any other, Jesus was not a Man concerned with what men could do to Him, and He was even less concerned with what they could do *for* Him. His singular concerns were

truth,
> right, and
>> His Father's will.

Those moneychangers and merchants, along with the religious leaders who participated with them, were all getting rich. Religious manipulation and commercialization were as profitable then as they are, well, today—Father God, blatantly exploited for personal gain!

What a ghastly desecration. What a grievous affront. And what a deep and personal wound it must have been for Jesus!

So like a monolith of virtue, Jesus takes the stand that no one else would. In defense of the living God, in defense of all that is pure and good, He rises like a tower of truth and marches headlong into the heat of that place where no other man had the guts to go.

Can you imagine the heavenly roar in His holy voice as He belted that day, "*How dare you turn My Father's house into a market!*" (John 2:16). Glory to His blessed Name!

I have to suppose there were many men over the years who'd seen the same atrocities that Jesus saw and were equally horrified. Perhaps they'd joked sarcastically, with some degree of discomfort, "God sure is good business." I wonder how many of those men, year after year, watched as one or another religious merchant took a widow's last dime. I wonder how many stood by and said nothing.

The priests, scribes, and teachers of the law were men too. They knew the wrong that was going on; a blind man could see it. Instead of taking a stand, however, many participated and even profited, and I can only guess at the spirituality they massaged themselves with as they did so: "The worker is worth his wage, brother." "Praise God for the blessing!"

How opposite of Jesus! There He is, standing tall and brimming with manhood, high above them all. He alone takes the stand for holiness. He alone puts everything on the line for what everyone knows is right.

It's Jesus whose heart breaks to the point that He cannot sit still and do nothing. It's Jesus who rises to defend the widows and hoist the standard of God. It's Jesus who draws the line in the sand and belts across time and eternity, "No more! Never again!" Glory to the Name of Jesus!

Taking that kind of stand was Jesus's lifestyle two thousand years ago. It was His way every day. It was so very much who Jesus *was* that for Him to have acted in any other way would have been for Him to deny, well, Himself. To not rise up, to not defend righteousness, to not stand for good no matter the risk or opposition, would simply have been for Jesus to not be Jesus.

Maybe that's true for you and me, too, when we don't stand up. Maybe that's why failing to take a stand is so devastating to a man's manhood. Maybe that's why it causes such injury and shame. For a child of God not to step up to the plate in those kinds of moments is for that child of God to deny who he is. It's simply to be what a child of God is not.

Oh so tragically, a man keeps silent. He does nothing or, worse yet, does something to "go with the flow." As a result, unrighteousness, ungodliness, the enemy—His enemy, and yours and mine—wins. Oh, Father, have mercy!

There's another Jesus story I love that has to do with this same theme. It takes place during a peak in His ministry. He's just finished feeding the five thousand, His name is spreading like wildfire, and every day is filled with throngs upon throngs. "And a great crowd of people followed him because they saw the miraculous signs he had performed on the sick" (John 6:2).

On this particular day, Jesus is in a Capernaum synagogue, surrounded by who knows how many. No doubt the apostles are excited. All those long days of preaching on street corners, being scorned and rejected, are finally behind them. The "Jesus mania" they'd fasted and prayed for is finally happening!

There's great anticipation as Jesus rises to teach. The buzz rippling through the crowd turns to sudden quiet. Everyone leans in, not wanting to miss even one of His words: "I tell you the truth, unless you eat the flesh of the Son of Man and drink his blood, you have no life in you. Whoever eats my flesh and drinks my blood has eternal life, and I will raise him up at the last day. For my flesh is real food and my blood is real drink. Whoever eats my flesh and drinks my blood remains in me, and I in him. Just as the living Father sent me and I live because of the Father, so the one who feeds on me will live because of me" (John 6:53–57).

Oh—my—goodness. "Eats my flesh"? Drinks my blood"? "My flesh is food"? "The one who feeds on me will live"?

In God's holy Name—pun fully intended—*what grisly horror is this Guy talking about?*

As you and I look back through the glasses of so much teaching to what we know those words mean, we say, "Of course." But imagine hearing them on that day. "The pews" got suddenly *very* empty. "From this time many of his disciples turned back and no longer followed him" (John 6:66). So much for the great revival. So much for "Jesus mania."

Again, *Jesus knew.* Again, He was no dummy. He knew that once He spoke those words, there would be few survivors, if any. He knew all that and then some—*and He did it anyway.*

After all, the truth is the truth, and sometimes that's the price a guy has to pay to stand in truth. Sometimes that's the price a guy has to pay to

speak truth,

uphold truth,

and day by day walk it out.

Sometimes that's the price a guy has to pay to honor his God and live life in a way that truly pleases Him. *Sometimes that's what it costs for a man to be all the man he can possibly be.*

To Jesus two thousand years ago, there was no gray zone. There was no flip-flopping about these things. There was no "Where's the balance?" or "Yeah, but . . ." There was no "winning friends and influencing people," no "fitting in," no "getting ahead."

To Jesus there was just

truth,

righteousness,

holiness.

There was just, "Better is one day in your courts than a thousand elsewhere" (Psalm 84:10). "Choose . . . this day whom you will serve" (Joshua 24:15). "I would rather be a doorkeeper in the house of my God than dwell in the tents of the wicked" (Psalm 84:10).

There was just "Dad" and Dad alone. There was just knowing Dad as He fully was. There was just living each and every day as the Man His Dad purposed Him to be.

The fear of the LORD is the beginning of wisdom,
and knowledge of the Holy One is understanding.
—Proverbs 9:10

What good will it be for a man if he gains the whole world, yet forfeits his soul? Or what can a man give in exchange for his soul?
—Matthew 16:26

Glory to the Name of Jesus!

It must surely make Jesus dance circles around His throne to see men and women who stand for God and draw the line as Jesus did.

I close this chapter with stories of two men who inspire us all to be like the Man Jesus. The bar Jesus set two thousand years ago is so incredibly high that a guy can easily sink into thinking, *Why am I even trying?* But then, to realize there are guys no different than you and I who are out there "doing it"! Yes, they stumble like all of us, but at least now and again they actually approach the bar. Glory to the Name of Jesus!

The first story took place years ago, when I was on a kinda-sorta double date with a dear friend, Bruce Rudnick. All through our precious friendship, Bruce has humbled me with the depth of his love for Jesus and his total lack of compromise. I'm not sure I've ever met a man with more compassion for people, more joy in the Lord, and more willingness to be a "fool" for Jesus in human eyes.

We were in Johannesburg, South Africa, and the four of us went to the movies. Bruce and both girls were real artists—painters, sculptors—so, as you might expect, they chose an "art" movie. That, of course, means it was a foreign film as opposed to an American one. It was French or maybe Italian; I don't remember. We'd all heard it was a good movie—a real human drama, as European movies tend to be. And as far as any of us knew, there was nothing immoral about it. So we bought our tickets, loaded up on popcorn, and took our seats.

The lights dimmed.

Hardly fifteen minutes passed before it became very clear this film was going where we, as children of God, had no business going. There was nothing blatantly immoral on the screen. People weren't taking off their clothes, having sex, or anything like that. It was more the "undercurrent"—dark, moody, and anything but godly.

To be honest with you, we should have known. As I said, it was a European art film—what more did we need to know? European filmmakers and actors are expert in making the air in a theater as thick as mud. They know how to "say" more with a look or a pause or a camera angle than all the in-your-face stuff of typical American movies combined.

So there we were, fifteen minutes into it, and we knew we were headed for trouble. All of us knew it—*but Bruce was the one who did something about it.*

Bruce and I were sitting shoulder to shoulder with each

of the girls on our opposite sides. There was uncomfortable silence across the theater and a sense of uncomfortable conviction among us four.

Suddenly Bruce jumped from his chair as if he'd been jabbed with a needle. "Well, I've had just about enough of this," he announced, as big as an announcement can be. He turned to his date and excused himself. He said he'd be waiting for her outside. Then he slipped past my knees and walked out the back door. Welcome to Bruce Rudnick!

A few minutes later I slipped out myself to look for him. He was sitting in a sidewalk café across the street, sipping a cappuccino. It was a beautiful summer night with the world of South African city life sauntering by at that oh so mellow African pace. I sat down with Bruce and ordered a cappuccino for myself.

I remember his words as we sat there. I remember them *exactly*, because they so struck me: *"I'm a child of God, Bruce. I don't need to subject myself to that."*

It was such a humble, virile, righteous statement. Here was a man with clear understanding of what honored God and what didn't, what was "of Him" and what wasn't. A man entirely unafraid of what I, those girls, or anyone else in that theater might think of him. A man willing to risk ridicule and rejection for love of His Father and His Father's ways.

That night Bruce was also a man who valued himself. He was a man who understood who he was as a man: *a son of*

God. He understood what was profitable for his soul and what wasn't, what would bless and what would tear down, what would draw him closer to His Father and to the man His Father called him to be, and what would make those very challenging pursuits all the more difficult.

That night Bruce understood—and he took a stand. He took a "Jesus stand." Glory to the Name of Jesus!

Bruce and I shared many cappuccinos that night. We sat for nearly two hours, waiting for the girls while they watched the entire movie. But we didn't mind. We just enjoyed our cappuccinos and cake. We laughed and told stories and had the absolute time of our lives.

We were two sons of God sitting on an African sidewalk, basking in the twin joys of His love for both of us and our brotherhood in the arms of Jesus. Glory to His Name!

My second story has to do with a singer/songwriter who's dancing joyously right alongside Jesus today—a guy we all knew and loved through his music, Rich Mullins. I never met Rich personally, but from every story I've ever heard about him, I think I would have appreciated him a whole lot.

I don't remember the occasion, but one time I was sitting with a well-known contemporary Christian music artist, and Rich's name came up. It may have been around the time of his death several years ago; I don't know. I was curious and asked this woman if she knew Rich. She said she'd only met him once. Then her face smiled big, and she told me this story.

Rich was set to perform his famous "Awesome God" at one of those giant conventions where everyone who's anyone in terms of Christian music, books, or films gathers a couple of times a year. I can't remember if it was the Gospel Music Association Awards or the Christian Booksellers Association Convention; suffice it to say, it was *big*. The auditorium was loaded with Christian record producers, publishing CEOs, agents, and distributors, not to mention lots of artists and press.

The fact that Rich was performing was all the buzz. The house was packed, and everyone was there to see him.

Rich stepped onto the stage in his typical jeans and flannel shirt. Apparently Rich was the kind of guy who didn't "put on a show" for anyone. He downplayed himself infamously, always doing everything he could to make sure God received the glory.

The place "went bananas" with applause. It seemed to take forever for everyone to calm down. Rich just sat at the piano, waiting, and then he began to play and sing of the awesomeness, love, and power of our almighty God.

Rich sang and sang, and God was lifted up and up. I can only imagine the glory that must have flooded that room. He played and he sang, and eventually he played his last note.

When he was done, the room immediately erupted in a

veritable volcano of applause. The audience jumped to their feet, whistling and hooting and clapping like mad. It was a standing ovation in honor of Rich and his musical legacy—a literal *explosion* of acclaim and excitement that went on and on.

As the story was told to me, Rich just sat there quietly at the piano, his head down, waiting for it all to be over. Minutes passed, and still they applauded. Finally the clamor ceased, and Rich was still sitting there.

The room went silent.

Rich turned his head, looked out at the audience, leaned into his microphone, and spoke these mind-blowing, self-dethroning, God-exalting, fearing-no-man words: *"You people just don't get it, do you?"*

Then he stood, walked out the stage door, jumped in his Jeep, and drove away.

Rich had written that song for one purpose and one purpose only: to glorify the living God. He'd written those lyrics to inspire a healthy and holy fear of God—to lead men and women to understand how truly awesome God is, so that they might fall on their faces and lay their lives at His glorious feet. Oh, glory to His Name!

That night the people had the opportunity to do that—the opportunity to worship their awesome God. The song called them to lift their voices and their hands. It was a veritable trumpet blast inviting them to drop to their knees before His most magnificent throne.

The song offered them God, God, and more God—but they were more interested in Rich. They applauded Rich. They gave Rich the glory. They walked right by the living God in their fascination with a man.

Apparently that fascination was something Rich wasn't interested in and couldn't sit still for. It was wrong. There's no place for such things in the kingdom of God.

I'm going to guess a lot of people were insulted by Rich that night—a lot of "big" people in the worlds of Christian publishing and recording. But Rich was not a man concerned with the bigness or smallness of anyone. He was a man singularly concerned with God, and He had to take a stand for Him—for Him who *alone* deserves the glory.

Just like Jesus in those temple courts, Rich just *had* to say something. Rich had to "be Jesus."

You people just don't get it, do you?"

"I've had just about enough of this."

"How dare you turn my Father's house into a market!"

A guy named Rich, a guy named Bruce, and a Man beyond men named Jesus. Glory to the Name of Jesus!

A MAN OF SELFLESSNESS

The Gospels of Jesus Christ—every story of Jesus and His every word and action within them—when refined to their purest essence, chronicle the same, most breathtaking reality over and over: the Son of the living God *giving Himself away*.

It's so startling in its simplicity that one could easily say, "No, it couldn't be." But then you open your Bible. You turn page after page of Matthew, Mark, Luke, and John. You look, you read, and it's *everywhere*: Jesus giving, and then giving even more.

"When Jesus landed and saw a large crowd, he had compassion on them and healed their sick" (Matthew 14:14). "Jesus said to him, 'I will go and heal him'" (Matthew 8:7). "Filled with compassion, Jesus reached out his hand and touched the man. 'I am willing,' he said. 'Be clean!'" (Mark 1:41).

"The good shepherd lays down his life for the sheep" (John 10:11). "I am going there to prepare a place for you" (John 14:2). "And when Jesus had cried out again in a loud voice, he gave up his spirit" (Matthew 27:50). "And surely I am with you always, to the very end of the age" (Matthew 28:20).

"Here's my truth," Jesus said over and over. "I give you My truth. Take it for your own.

"Here's

My power,
　　My leadership,
　　　　My sweat,
　　　　　　My tears.

Here's food for the hungry, eyes for the blind, legs for the lame, ears for the deaf. Here's life for the dead and buried, and life abundant for the dead who aren't yet buried. Take them all—it's why I've come. Take them as your own.

"I've shed My glory for you, My child; My peace I give to you. Yes, even My blood I give to you, that you may find rest for your precious, precious soul."

JESUS!

Two thousand years ago, Jesus's way of life was to give His life away. It was what He did when He walked away from the glories of His heavenly throne, and what He did when He walked away from the securities of His Nazareth home. It was what He did when He stood in the marketplaces and poured out His heart, and what He did when He bent down to lift a blind beggar from his darkness or a bleeding woman from her despair.

Giving is what Jesus did when He curled up in whatever field or on whatever floor and whispered Himself to sleep, praying for you and me. Giving was what He did when He stood before Pontius Pilate and, oh so breathtakingly, said absolutely *nothing*.

Giving Himself away *was* Jesus. It was what

He lived to do,
>>what He loved to do,
>>>what He was born to do,
>>>>and what He died doing.

It was the heartbeat of His every teaching, His every miracle, His every drop of blood, and every moment of His glorious return.

Jesus, if I may, was "living giving." Giving *alive*. The human perfection of selflessness.

Selflessness is a theme—a Jesus reality—that dovetails with other themes we've explored, most especially humility. It's impossible to discuss one without the other. But therein is the testimony to the centrality of selflessness within the character of Jesus: His "everything else" was woven into it and born out of it.

His passion as a Man, His devotion to His Father, His care and respect for women, His graciousness in speech,

His graciousness in conduct and, indeed, His masculine excellence: selflessness was the hub, the golden key, the indisputable reality that lay at the root of them all.

There's a problem with selflessness and giving, though. To begin with, is there anything that grates against human nature more? Is there anything that is more opposite to the macho maxims of dominance, drive, and ambition? Is there anything more contrary to "the way of the world"? Is there anything more challenging to a man than self-sacrifice?

It's no mystery that giving has also been heartbreakingly warped and cheapened by religious manipulations that beat the drum into the ground while they beat people over the head. That which is so pure and holy, so central to Jesus, and so pivotal for a man in terms of modeling Jesus, is so often tragically abused, and (I'll just say it) prostituted.

It's all an otherworldly strategy that dates back two thousand years, singularly aimed at "defacing" Jesus—blinding people to who He truly is, distorting His "features," if you will.

"Just as there were many who were appalled at him—his appearance was so disfigured beyond that of any man and his form marred beyond human likeness" (Isaiah 52:14). Yes, the Enemy "went for it" physically that day on Golgotha, and he's still going for it today in the hearts and minds of people. He takes those things that are Jesus's beauty, those things that are His "face," and he mars them so that many turn away from Jesus.

The Enemy buries grace beneath rules and traditions. He twists compassion to look like weakness. He dirties love with dirty things, and imposes pride and piety on holiness.

It's actually quite remarkable what he does to giving. He paints over its wonder with hard colors and twisted hues that somehow make it look more like, well, *being taken*.

On the other side of all that distortion is purity of truth and unaltered reality—"two thousand years ago" reality . . .

A Man stands at an ancient crossroads, sweating in the heat of the afternoon sun, belting out His life-saving truths for any passerby who would care to listen. A Man weeps in the temple courtyard over the lostness of His "children," then rises to His feet to heal them. A Man hangs on a piece of wood and breathes His last.

JESUS.

Yes, there is pure truth and unaltered reality to be realized and held in one's heart, that truth, that reality, is *giving*. It's the reality of a Man entirely void of self, who spends His every day pouring His everything into other people, laying His every resource and every treasure at their undeserving feet.

Picture, if you will, Jesus, in the middle of the night on the Mount of Olives, shivering in the cold and praying for people who will call for His death and spit in His face. Picture Jesus feeding hungry masses, washing people's feet, lifting a widow's son from the cold of his coffin, and lifting Himself onto the horror of a tree.

> There's no provision for self,
>> no allegiance to self,
>>> no balance between giving and keeping.

There's only care—desperate, all-out, unrestrained *care*.

There's only passion for people and passion for the Father—and all the selflessness and sacrifice that goes with it. There's only giving, giving, and more giving.

JESUS!

I think of the ten lepers that Jesus healed two thousand years ago—ten men to whom He gave of His divine resources for the purpose of making their bodies whole (Luke 17:11–19). Jesus miraculously and breathtakingly healed them. In the blink of an eye, He freed each and every one of them from the hell of sickened and deformed bodies. He hoisted them from blackened pits of human worthlessness and catapulted them into wholeness and value. He restored them to their families, their homes, their friends, their jobs.

The compound and multiple layers of what Jesus gave these men that miraculous day went so far beyond mere physical healing. He gave them "hope and a future" (Jeremiah 29:11). He turned their "mourning into dancing" (Psalm 30:11 NKJV). He wiped "every tear from their eyes" and ensured no more "crying or pain" (Revelation 21:4). *And only one of them returned to say, "Thank you."*

That's a shocking fact, I know. But it's not what's *really* shocking. It's not what *really* blows the mind and totally, completely mystifies.

What *really* blows the mind is that Jesus knew that would happen. He was the Son of the living God; He knew the hearts of these men. He knew they wouldn't thank Him. He knew they were taking advantage of Him.

It's not just that they didn't honor Him as Lord—they treated Him like dirt. They used Him. They "took the money and ran" without even throwing Him a token of basic decency.

But He healed them anyway! Oh, revelation beyond revelations of the selfless heart of Jesus! *He gave Himself to them anyway*.

JESUS.

What a picture of the canyon between human nature and His nature, man's ways and His ways. What a glaring display of the self-centered heart of man, and right alongside it, right in the middle of it, wrapping arms of care all around it, the wholesale selflessness of Jesus.

From moment number one these men were all about themselves, *but He healed them anyway*. They couldn't have cared less about Jesus or His Father's kingdom, *and He healed them anyway*. When they called Him "Master," it was nothing more than a pitiful manipulation—how terribly mocking!—*and He healed them anyway*.

He loved them, and so He healed them. Glory to the Name of Jesus!

There was one man, however, who did return to say thank you that day. Oh, blessed, blessed one!

I don't know exactly where Jesus may have been when the man approached. For some reason I picture Jesus in a somewhat quiet place, maybe on the outskirts of the village, maybe resting with the apostles after another long day.

Maybe it was late afternoon or early evening. Perhaps some of Jesus's companions were lying around napping, others off fishing. Maybe there was something cooking on the fire as they all settled in for the night.

I picture Jesus very quiet that afternoon. He'd been going from village to village, pouring Himself out, day after exhausting day bringing Him a lifetime of joys and a lifetime of heartaches. He's sitting on a rock or a stump or something, off to Himself, maybe repairing the leather on one of His sandals or stirring the coals on the fire.

Enter the one leper who returns. All afternoon this man has been looking at his hands and feeling his face. What happened is just so beyond unbelievable! He can feel the strength that has been restored to his muscles; he can see the looks of wonder in everyone else's eyes.

His wife just cried and cried when he went to her. Oh, how she cried! And his kids—they ran to him and climbed all over him. They couldn't get enough of him, nor he of them. It was all so beyond unbelievable!

The man is out of breath with excitement and all the day's emotion as he runs up and falls to the ground at Jesus's feet. He stumbles in speechlessness, so unable to convey even a corner of all that's bursting inside him.

In precious awkwardness, he trips and fumbles over his brand-new tongue. He can't remember any of the speech he'd prepared, and so it just gushes out of him, the only words he can find to say: "Thank You, thank You! Praise God! Thank You!"

Jesus just smiles. Gently, quietly, regally, He smiles. Tears begin to well in His eyes. They're *real* tears—tears that bulb and fall and pool in the sand beneath Him. They're tears of love for this one man and tears of love for the nine others. They're tears for the way the nine broke His heart and tears for the way one mended it.

Perhaps Jesus reaches out a hand to him. Perhaps He strokes his hair or cups his face. Then the words—almost a whisper: "Were not all ten cleansed?" It's so quiet, so still. The man lifts his eyes to meet Jesus's, so ashamed for those others. "Where are the other nine?"

JESUS.

Then came the day that Jesus hung from a tree outside Jerusalem. Guessing that those nine men were there, I wonder if there was a moment when Jesus looked down and somehow, through the swelling of His shredded eyelids, locked eyes with them.

I wonder if they laughed in His face or stood frozen and speechless. I wonder if each of them had a woman tucked under one arm and a pint of whatever swinging from the other, or if they were flat on their faces, crying tears for what they had done.

I don't know—no one can know. But I do know *He died for them anyway.*

For God so loved the world that he gave his one and only Son, that whoever believes in him shall not perish but have eternal life.
—John 3:16

Greater love has no one than this, that he lay down his life for his friends.
—John 15:13

And when Jesus had cried out again in a loud voice, he gave up his spirit.
—Matthew 27:50

The Cross.

The self-sacrifice.

The "giving Himself away"

like no one has ever given himself away.

Yes, there's giving, and then there's Golgotha. There's self-lessness, *and then there's Jesus.*

Two thousand years ago a Man named Jesus stood in the marketplaces and on the hillsides of ancient Israel, sweat rolling down His face, tears spilling off His holy cheeks. All day long, with everything He was, He cared for people, led people, fed people; He healed their sick and raised their dead.

Day after day He lifted them from lives lived in the dirt, and night after night He laid His own head to sleep in the sand. Day after day He called their lives into eternities of heavenly goodness, then one afternoon He laid His own life before all of hell's horror. With everything He was, quite simply, He gave away everything He was.

JESUS.

When I was a kid I did all sorts of odd jobs to earn a buck where I could. One of my favorite jobs in those days was valet parking for a five-star restaurant. Its doors closed years ago, but in its day it was rated among the finest restaurants in the nation.

The job was really a whole lot of fun. Just being outdoors and meeting interesting folks was great. Then every night my friends would come and visit, and we'd sit outdoors together and enjoy the Southern California evenings.

And of course, there were the cars. There I was, just a teenager, driving Ferraris, Lamborghinis, Rolls-Royces, you name it. I'm convinced the whole reason I never had that typical guy fascination with cars (and the reason I'm happy today with anything that gets me around) is because I wore it out on that job. I'd been to the "car mountain" so many times, I got bored with it!

One of the folks who came to the restaurant for dinner now and again was Chuck Swindoll, the well-known Christian author. At the time I had no idea who he was. I wasn't born again back in those days and had no interest in being born again, so I had no basis for knowing him. All I knew was there was this man who drove an older BMW—a nice car, but nothing showy. He was always with his wife, and they were always holding hands, and they just seemed like a neat couple.

But here's the thing: this guy was always *so* nice to me. As you can imagine, a lot of people don't give the valet guy much attention, so when someone treats you nicely, you really notice it.

Every time this man got out of his car, he would turn and ask me sincerely how I was doing, and then we'd have a little chat. I felt as if he actually, sincerely cared. *Like Jesus*, I guess, he would stop everything and take time for me—a nothing, nobody parking attendant. Nice, isn't it?

One time he drove up, and again he did his usual: he stopped to chat with me. Then he took his wife by the hand, and they went into the restaurant. I was so taken, I wanted to know more about him. So I looked through the window of the BMW into the backseat, and there it was: a big, black, leather-bound Bible.

I remember seeing that Bible, and thinking to myself, *This guy is one of those born-again Christians.* Then I went to the hostess and asked to see the reservation sheet—again, I wanted to know who he was. I looked, and there was his name scratched in pencil: "C. Swindoll, party of two."

I never forgot that in the years that followed. As you can see, I remember it in detail to this day. Since coming to Jesus and growing in the ministry He's given me, I've often thought, *Someday I'm going to run into Chuck and I'll tell him that story.* I think it will surely bless him as he so blessed me—*as he so modeled Jesus* to a lost parking attendant in a mangy bow tie, planting a precious kingdom seed that would take root and blossom in years to come. Thanks, Chuck. Glory to Jesus!

There was another guy who was a regular diner at that restaurant. As far as I know, he wasn't a guy who knew Jesus as his Savior, though I could be wrong. I know he was a surgeon—

very well respected. A major hospital was just up the street, and he and his partners came in regularly at the end of their days. We always rolled out the red carpet for them; we knew they worked so very hard, and their work was so very important.

Some of the partners were a little on the flamboyant side. Some of them had eyes for the girls and enjoyed the high life, but not this doctor. He was the quiet one. He was the family man who conducted himself with dignity and reserve. He was a gracious man, feet on the ground; a very solid man, calm and sure. He was always the one to leave the restaurant first—the one who said, "I have to get home."

This may seem a funny thing to remember, but I have good reason to mention it: this doctor had two cars. He had a little Mercedes SL sports car that was his "everyday" car. It was the car he always drove when he came in for dinner with his partners or after work for hors d'oeuvres.

His other car was a bigger car. It was a sedan; if memory serves, it was a Lincoln, though I'm not sure. That was his "take his wife out to dinner" car.

You see, his wife had had a stroke or an accident or was battling cancer—I don't remember exactly what the problem was, but I know it was no small matter. She probably would have preferred the SL, but her mobility was somewhat limited. So the good doctor had this other car—*for her*.

This doctor was a relatively young man—another odd fact to mention, but important to the story. I distinctly remember thinking, *Man, this guy really has the world on a string.* He was handsome, successful, and respected. He wasn't flighty or showy, like so many of his peers. He didn't flash his wealth or demand special attention. He was just a rich, gracious, good-hearted, handsome, young man.

In other words, this was a man whom women would typically be lining up for, and as I watched from the anonymity of my parking-attendant status, that's exactly what women were doing. Hey, who could blame them?

But all those wannabes had a problem: the doctor wasn't interested in the least. He had this wife—this wife who wasn't well, who hadn't been well for a long time, who would never get well, and whose remaining wellness was deteriorating with each passing day. He had this wife he deeply loved and to whom he was deeply devoted, despite her condition. He would never even think of violating her in any way.

I remember the two of them came in for dinner by themselves almost every Saturday night. That sedan would roll into my parking lot, and I'd hustle over to the passenger door, open it wide, and smile big. Knowing that things weren't going well, I always did my best to handle the doctor's wife with extra care, taking her hand and helping her out of the car.

And the doctor was so good to her. Never once did I see him walk ahead of her into the restaurant, no matter how slow she got as time went on. He always opened the door for her. He'd take her arm and kind of support her, and then he'd just melt into her pace in an easy, subtle way that didn't let on to her what he was doing.

I watched that couple countless times over the years I worked as a valet, and countless times I watched that doctor treat his wife like his most precious, most treasured, most beloved queen. There wasn't one time I saw him with her—*or even without her*, if you know what I mean—that he didn't handle her with the utmost respect, the utmost care, the utmost tenderness, the utmost value. I watched her worsen and worsen, months into years, and I watched her husband treat her like his queen.

Inevitably, the day came when the big sedan didn't roll in every Saturday anymore. The day came when I drove it less and less—every other Saturday, every third Saturday, every other month. Then the day came when I only drove his SL on weekdays. Now and again the sedan would pull in for some birthday or special occasion, but it was always just him with the kids. Mom was too sick to go out anymore. And then one day Mom was no more.

Here was a man who could have gone so many other ways. He had more options, if you will, than most men could dream of—kind of like Jesus, I guess. But what he chose to do was give his life away. He loved his bride so much that he gave his life away . . . to her.

That was many years ago, and that doctor is remarried today. God has blessed him with a new bride, and if I know anything about God, she's a very special woman—a real "reward," if I may put it that way, for a man who, though he may or may not be born again, surely understands care and goodness, righteousness and commitment, selflessness and all the wonders that go with it.

And if that doctor is anything like he used to be way back when I parked his cars and wore a little bow tie, I can promise you his wife is one very happy woman. She's one very blessed bride.

Selflessness. Giving. They lay at the heart of Jesus's manhood two thousand years ago. They lay at the heart of His hope for men today.

Jesus, Jesus, Jesus. Glory to the Name of Jesus!

A Man of the Spirit

But if I drive out demons by the Spirit of God,
then the kingdom of God has come upon you.
~Matthew 12:28

The people were amazed at his teaching,
because he taught them as one who had authority,
not as the teachers of the law.
~Mark 1:22

And with that he breathed on them and said,
"Receive the Holy Spirit."
~John 20:22

Two thousand years ago Jesus lived and moved, worked and taught, made His day-to-day choices and His year-to-year decisions, by the leadership, strengthening, equipping, and upholding *of the Holy Spirit.*

Jesus was conceived in the power of the Holy Spirit

(Luke 1:35). He "grew in wisdom and stature, and in favor with God and men" (Luke 2:52) and by the instruction and discipline of the Holy Spirit. "Everyone who heard him was amazed at his understanding and his answers" (Luke 2:47), which came from the inspiration of the Holy Spirit. He stepped where the Spirit told Him to step and went only where the Spirit pointed Him to go.

Everything Jesus did and every word He spoke was born of the Spirit of God. The Spirit was His sustenance, His life force, if you will. It was His equipping for both the extraordinary and the day-to-day. It was His Father's whisper to the ears of His heart and His Father's embrace around the ache in His heart. It was the Rock He leaned on when He could go no further and the joy song he danced to in victory.

The Spirit of Truth,
the Spirit of His Father,
the Counselor,
the Comforter

—the almighty Spirit of our most breathtaking God. Glory to His magnificent Name!

People often get a little nervous when it comes to the Holy Spirit and discussions of the Holy Spirit, and for good reason. Let's face it—so much teaching says one thing about Him, and so much teaching says the complete opposite, that many folks just don't know what to believe.

On the one hand, there are lines of doctrine that downplay and even disregard the Spirit, often planting fear of Him in people's hearts. On the other hand, there is that, shall I say, "odd" behavior and flamboyant talk that so often comes from the "other camp" and scares people just as well. The end result is that a lot of precious people are confused and caught in the middle. Oh, what a heartbreaking reality!

The Holy Spirit is God, *period*. It really is that pure, that wonderful, and that simple. He's the third Person of the Trinity, the Three-in-One, Triune God—the mirror reality of the Father, and the mirror reality of Jesus.

His participation in a person's day-to-day life is as practical and unscary a consideration as a consideration can be. So much so, that for a person to pursue life without Him would be like a construction worker going to a work site without his toolbox. The Holy Spirit really is that *real*, that "feet on the ground," and anything but bizarre as He is sometimes represented to be.

And, of course, rising like a monolith of truth in the midst of all the untruth that would seek to confuse is Jesus. I picture Him rising from the ground of all that creates confusion and fear like a granite horn of rock-solid reality—the living testimony to who the Holy Spirit *truly* is, and what is truly the Spirit's hope for a man's life.

He stands majestic in humility, triumphant in servitude—

the human model of what the Holy Spirit is able to form in a man. He stands meek in integrity, joyous in suffering—the living evidence of the Spirit's power in the life of a man. He stands

> emboldened for righteousness,
>> equipped for the miraculous,
>>> impassioned for human souls

—the ultimate expression of the Spirit's purpose for a man. He stands glorious in character, excellent in manhood—the pinnacle presentation of the living Spirit of the living God, wholly living in a whole and living man. Glory to the Name of Jesus!

Two thousand years ago, Jesus was sealed in righteousness by the strengthening and faithfulness of the Holy Spirit. He was forged as "a weapon fit for its work" (Isaiah 54:16) by the blacksmithing hands of the Holy Spirit. His endurance and stamina, His focus and drive, His determination to press on no matter what, was all powered by the girding up of the Holy Spirit.

His faithfulness and confidence, joy and compassion, were sculpted into Him by the carving of the Holy Spirit. His quality of manhood was shaped and defined, perfected and completed, by the *true* manliness He learned in union with the Spirit.

A MAN OF THE SPIRIT

As a living, breathing Man in the streets and alleyways of ancient Israel, Jesus *lived* the Holy Spirit. It wasn't something that came and went and made Him act "goofy." It wasn't something He "conjured up" when He needed a miracle. The Holy Spirit was His constant and dearest companion. The Holy Spirit was His confidant, His advisor, His moment-by-moment leader and the source He looked to for meeting His every hope and need. The Holy Spirit, quite simply, was the totality of His Father given complete access and operating fully in every corner of His most blessed life.

And the Holy Spirit's objective within the Person of Jesus was no different than His objective in you or me: to hand-carry Him into the fullest fulfillment of everything He was born to be. To be there for Him and equip Him, to fill His heart and mind with His Father's thinking, priorities, and ways. To supply every resource, He needed to fulfill His Father's plan and manifest His Father's kingdom. To so occupy and consume His life that not a moment would be wasted in angst, insecurity, or unworthy pursuits.

Because Jesus understood all of this and more, He had one remarkably simple and singular approach to life, one key to success, if you will, one triumphant answer that was the summation of His life: *He entirely lived in, entirely depended upon, and entirely followed the Holy Spirit.* It was Jesus's formula for perfection of life and life lived in perfection.

CHAPTER EIGHT

Don't you believe that I am in the Father,
and that the Father is in me? The words I say to you
are not just my own. Rather, it is the Father,
living in me, who is doing his work.
—John 14:10

Can you imagine the kind of confidence and liberation that comes with *completely* depositing your life into the Father's Spirit hands? Can you imagine

the security,

the certainty,

the freedom from

"What if *this?*" and "What if *that?*"

You just hear Him and go. "God's heart is for me, not against me," you say. "I need only go." Glory to the Name of Jesus!

Yes, Jesus's life was really so incredibly simple—never easy, but always simple. Every moment was, "What does My Dad want Me to do now?" That was His total motivation and life plan—a plan that walked Him straight into His greatest fulfillment, His greatest victories, and the perfection of everything He could be. "What does My Dad want Me to do?" Glory to the Name of Jesus!

At once the Spirit sent him out into the desert" (Mark 1:12).

As I said, "never easy." Barely dry from His Jordan baptism, the Spirit of God whispered, "Follow Me."

The challenge wasn't as big as one might think, though. Who among us wouldn't have jumped up immediately after what the Holy Spirit had just done? As Luke 3:21–22 recounts, the Spirit had just exploded over that baptismal scene in indescribable magnificence. He'd literally breached the physical world with His supernatural glory—so much so that Scripture says people actually saw Him.

And how did they describe what they saw—or perhaps, more accurately, *felt*—that day? It was so far beyond what any of them had ever come close to feeling, or seeing.

"There was

this 'reality,'
　this 'abiding,'
　　this 'Person'

—yes, that's it!—that I couldn't actually see, but I knew He was real, because He was so *there*.

"At the same time, I *could* see; it sounds funny, but He was like a dove. He hung over Jesus, and I couldn't even breathe because the joy was so thick. And all the human pain that I didn't even know was pain but thought was just normal life—it was so completely and entirely *gone*.

"Everything inside of me came alive as if for the first time. It was like my heart was dancing and my soul could finally breathe—as if in all the years I thought I was alive, I was more like dead.

"Yes, that's it! It was like *life itself was a living Person*! Life and goodness, wholeness and holiness, happiness and freedom, security and hope—they weren't 'concepts,' but *a Person*—and that Person was *alive*!

"Then there was that voice. I never heard anything like that voice in my life! In all the deepest recesses and highest heights of human eloquence, there's nothing that compares. It was so beyond huge—so soul-shaking and overwhelming, and at the same time, it was as intimate and private as a whisper. And it wasn't scary in the least. The awesomeness wasn't threatening at all. Its thunder was nothing but warm and good—*so* warm and *so* good that my knees went weak.

"And the love—oh, the love! Yes, that's it: the voice was like thunder, *and the voice was love*."

That voice, that thunderous whisper, asked Jesus to follow. And Jesus followed. He followed straight into forty days of the most life-crushing wilderness of "hell on earth." That same Spirit that had so honored Jesus at the Jordan now pointed Him to the desert and simply said, "Go."

There isn't too much known about Jesus in those forty

days. We know He didn't eat, though He easily could have, and being 100 percent human, He undoubtedly would have liked to. I can't imagine what it's like to literally starve, while having all the resources of the universe at your fingertips. I can't imagine what it's like to feel your face blister from day upon day of element upon element and not lift a finger against it. What a breathtaking depth of Spirit surrender!

And we must make no mistake—it truly was a living hell out there. There was nothing "religious" about it, if you know what I mean. Those forty days were desolation in every way, with the devil dangling every oasis of escape imaginable before Him.

"Come on, Man, just a bite," he essentially whispered to Jesus. "After all, You're the King of kings and Lord of lords. You're entitled, for crying out loud. Why wander around out here when You can have it all—*right now?*"

Can you imagine what the devil must have thrown at Jesus during those days? If you'll allow my imagination to run a bit, I picture him following Jesus around with a cornucopia of goodies, setting a table of finery just inches from His holy face. I picture him lying luxuriously at this gourmet-laden table, being shaded and fanned by some other filthy demon as all the other demons cater to his every whim.

They rush to clear his plates and bring him new ones. One demon massages his demon feet while another wipes the juice that spills over his demon chin. He waves the aromas of fresh bread and roasted lamb toward Jesus's divine nostrils, and he just smiles and enjoys and smiles . . .

"Don't sit there starving, good fellow. Your Father wouldn't *really* want You to starve now, would He? In fact—oh, please excuse me for talking with my mouth full; I know it's rude, but this is just so tasty—I've been thinking about this whole thing, and frankly, I think You may have heard the Spirit wrong. You're Messiah, for crying out loud. Shouldn't *You* be the one sitting at this table instead of me? Come on—just one bite."

But Jesus didn't take that bite, or any other bite. The Spirit had said no, and so He held on. No matter what, Jesus held on.

JESUS.

And what did Jesus do in those forty days while He held on? What did He do with all the nothingness upon nothingness? There was only blowing sand and baking rock; parched ground and endless desert;

> time,
>> silence,
>>> hunger,
>>>> and more time . . .

How did Jesus fill all that silence and solitude? How did He mark the morning after morning and nightfall after nightfall?

No one was there, so we can't say for sure, but my simple, unschooled guess is that He prayed. He prayed and He prayed and He prayed.

JESUS.

I picture Jesus seeking His Father with everything He is, crying out to Him. He weeps and wails, stretched out on His face. He casts Himself down, begging the Spirit to carry Him through. He thrusts His arms as high as starvation will take them. He throws back His head, and the tears flow.

"I love you, Father; I need You," He prays. "I love You; I need You."

JESUS.

I picture Him in the middle of the night, pressing as tightly as He can into a covey of boulders for whatever warmth they offer. I picture Him scraping pebbles and sand up around His shoulders and frame. I picture His body shaking hard to keep its temperature, His eyes searching the horizon for the warmth of sunrise.

His lips are frozen, yet He forces them open. They're too numb to feel, yet He pushes them to move. The words can't be heard over the wind that howls through the brush and explodes through the canyons, but they pour from His lips in a rush of need: "Oh Father, I'm Your Son! Father—Your Son!"

The daylight mercifully comes, but then the day cruelly peaks. The same sun that rescued Jesus from the cold now cranks His misery to the opposite extreme.

I picture Him pressed into those same boulders, but this time for shade. The desert heat is beating down, radiating up from the ground, then beating down again.

Still His lips move. Cracked and bleeding, they continue

their heavenly cry. As desperate as His circumstances are, that's how desperately He pleads; *that's how desperately He asks for more of His Father.*

As much as hunger claws at His belly, that's how hungrily He worships; that's how desperately He lifts His praise. As much as His tongue swells and His mouth turns to glue, that's how hard He presses in. As abandoned as His human reality insists that He is, that's how much He abandons Himself to His Father even more.

He falls to His knees afresh. He cries out again. He buries Himself in His Father's Spirit, wrapping it around His human weakness like a blanket around a freezing child. He pulls it tight, tight, ever-so-tight around

His heart,
    His mind,
        His flesh.

As the deer pants for streams of water,
so my soul pants for you, O God.
—Psalm 42:1

My soul yearns, even faints, for the courts of the LORD;
my heart and my flesh cry out for the living God.
—Psalm 84:2

Then He rises to His feet in a rush of fresh passion. His hands quake and quiver as He presses them skyward and bares

His palms. He shakes His mane free and roars, "Glory to You, Father!" in the face of all that roars against Him.

His name is Jesus, and He knows the fullness of all His name fully means: God saves, God saves, God saves! His name is Jesus, and He knows the fullness of all He was born to be and all He is as a Man in the grip of His Father's power and purpose. His name is Jesus, and He knows the fullness of all His Father is and all the glory and goodness that lie at His feet in the hands of His Father's Spirit.

Nothing is impossible in those hands, and Jesus knows it. No mountain is too high and no ocean too deep—it's all just a laugh in the hands of God! No forty days anywhere can knock a man out when he is upheld by the Holy Spirit. Let it be four hundred days! Bring it on!

There's no waste or weakness, no want or wilderness that can't be pushed through and overcome. Nothing is bigger than the living God—absolutely *nothing*—and Jesus *knows*.

JESUS!

*I will sing of the LORD's great love forever;
with my mouth I will make your faithfulness known.
—Psalm 89:1*

"You are more awesome than awesomeness itself," He cries. "Your right arm ripples with power and goodness; Your wonders never cease! You are My glory, O Father! Oh, to bathe in the perfume of Your Spirit! You are My strength, O God! Glory to Your wondrous Name!"

Yes, the Spirit of God led Jesus into hell on earth, and as mind-bending as it is to imagine, Jesus desired Him all the more. "Even though I walk through the valley of the shadow of death, I will fear no evil, for you are with me; your rod and your staff, they comfort me" (Psalm 23:4). "My heart is steadfast, O God; I will sing and make music with all my soul" (Psalm 108:1).

It is written, "Better is one day in your courts than a thousand elsewhere; I would rather be a doorkeeper in the house of my God than dwell in the tents of the wicked" (Psalm 84:10). These are words that Jesus, as the living God, "wrote" through one of His servants under the inspiration of His Holy Spirit hundreds of years earlier. By His Spirit once again, He literally lived them as a flesh-and-blood Man. He lived them every day of those forty days, every day that went before them, and every day that followed. He lived them all the way to Golgotha's tree.

"I would rather be a doorkeeper . . ."

JESUS.

Why would Jesus rather be that doorkeeper? Why does He choose to live those words? I'm no Bible scholar, but I can guess it's because they're true. I can guess it's because He knows that nothing else in life could even come close to "one day in your courts." There's no human comfort, wealth, wisdom, or leadership; no fulfillment of dreams; no anything or everything that can even begin to compare to life *in the hands of the Spirit of Abba Father*.

There's no depth of rest or pinnacle of peace; no greater guarantee of victory or value. There's

no treasure more dazzling,
> no involvement more joyous,
>> no security more sure.

There simply is no other place that Jesus would rather be.

So whether those "courts" mean wilderness hell or raising a little girl from the dead, Jesus goes. Whether being a "doorkeeper" means sawing wood for twenty years or driving demons into a herd of pigs, Jesus goes.

Whether "one day" is as spectacular as feeding thousands with a miracle or as ordinary as cooking for His friends on the beach; whether it's as supernatural as a "dove" descending in power, or as human as compassion for a widow who's lost her son—it's all the Holy Spirit, and it's all a whole lot better than anything and everything else; so Jesus simply goes.

Two thousand years ago, Jesus walked the path of the Holy Spirit's leadership and soared on the wings of His power. He danced in the courts of His counsel and swam in the oceans of His purpose. He leaned on the strength of His joy and wept in the grip of His sorrow. He stood tall in the excitement of His inspiration and stood even taller in the calm of His control.

As the Holy Spirit so fully lived in Jesus, so Jesus fully lived in Him. As the Holy Spirit so served Jesus, so Jesus served Him. As the Holy Spirit so guided, whispered into His ear, equipped and embraced, upheld and assured . . . so Jesus.

Jesus was the fullness of everything a man could possibly ever be, and that fullness was His Holy Spirit.

The Holy Spirit—Jesus. Jesus—the Holy Spirit. The living Spirit of His living Father, His own living Spirit, the living Holy Spirit. Jesus, Jesus, Jesus! Glory to the Name of Jesus!

I'm not one to tell stories about myself because, frankly, it feels weird to me when other people do the same thing. Whenever a man is the hero of his own stories, it seems, well, "yuck."

I can safely tell this story, though, because as much as it recounts a time when I rose to the occasion, there have been many more times I've fallen on my face. As much as it tells of how I clearly heard God and eventually responded, I can promise you, there have been many more times when I've missed Him. I'm as stumbling as anyone, and I'm just thankful for God's astounding mercy and redemption through all my foolishness and mistakes. Praise His wondrous Name!

A Man of the Spirit

It was an Easter Sunday, maybe four years ago. I had just wrapped up a thrilling but grueling morning of speaking at three different church services, and I was winding my way home through the vineyards and orchards of California's central coast.

The drive was absolutely beautiful. The California poppies were blooming, the sky was bluer than blue, and the fields were greener than green. Horses grazed in the pastures all around me. I thought back on the depth and quality of what God had done all morning. In every service there had been tears and more tears, and many folks had given their lives to Jesus. It was a spectacular day in every way.

The beauty around me and the privilege of participating in such exciting work was overwhelming that morning as I drove my way to a family celebration. I was a man living a dream life in the middle of a dream day, and I was so aware of it—and so very thankful to God. It was one of those times where you think, *Life doesn't get any better.* Little did I know that it was about to get "best."

I came around a bend, and there was a farmworker selling strawberries. That's a pretty typical sight in rural California—as humble and innocent a sight as can be. The man was all by himself, standing next to this old, beat-up car and a handmade sign with a funny kind of strawberry "face" painted on it. Flats of fresh strawberries were stacked on his trunk.

What happened next was so out-of-left-field and so

breathtakingly "of God," I can remember it like it was yesterday. As I turned to glance at the guy, it was as if God whispered to me, "I want you to share Jesus with that man." It's not that I heard an actual voice or anything. It's more that this *sense* rose in my heart, and it was so undeniably God. There could be no doubt I was "hearing" His heart for this precious man.

Well, I'm sorry to report that I wasn't too keen on that sense straight off. Forgive me, but it's one thing to share Jesus from a platform with a friendly congregation, and it's a whole other thing to share Him face to face with someone in the real world. I've done it countless times, but for some silly human reason, it can be a bit intimidating.

I also remember thinking, *Please, Lord, I've been at it all morning.* It was like telling your boss you'd already punched out. It's embarrassing to admit, but as I said, I'm just stumbling along like everyone else.

I actually drove past the man, but as you can guess, conviction crawled all over me. I was disobeying, and I knew it. I drove about a quarter of a mile and then finally caved in. I made a U-turn and went back—and oh, how I thank God for His grace and mercy!

This farmworker turned out to be the neatest guy. He was a middle-aged family man, and there were pictures of his wife and kids propped on the dashboard of his car. He didn't speak much English, but it was enough to mix with my bit of Spanish, and the two of us got on well.

I bought some strawberries, and he was thankful for that. Then, as I turned to leave, I blurted out, "*Amigo, tienes a Jesús en tu corazón?*" ("Friend, do you have Jesus in your heart?")

I will never forget the way he got very quiet and lowered his head. He was a physically strong man, maybe ten years my senior. His hands and arms were thick from years of physical labor. He had the kind of hands that could tear a phone book in half, yet he just got so quiet and soft.

His eyes misted, and he said nothing for the longest time. His humility was breathtaking. Then he slowly shook his head and simply answered, "No."

I wanted to take him in my arms, he was so very soft before God. In fact, I don't know that I've ever seen a man so soft before God.

He explained that his wife loved Jesus, but since he had to sell the strawberries on Sundays to earn a living, he was never able to go to church with her and their children. He said he needed God in his life and wanted God in his life. Then he absolutely blew my mind. He looked at me with the most innocent eyes and asked, "*Donde podre coneguir una Biblia?*" ("Where can I get a Bible?")

Oh, that moment! If ever I've recognized God's presence,

it was standing there on the road next to that man in that moment—more so than all the times I've stood in large auditoriums in worship. There was just silence, and he was so soft—this oh so precious man who was so dear to God that He had asked me to stop!

You can guess the rest of the story. I put the strawberries in my truck and pulled my Bible from my backpack. He didn't want to take it from me, but I insisted, and he finally said OK. Though he couldn't speak good English, he could read it well enough. I pointed him to a few key scriptures, prayed for him, and then I was on my way.

The next image is one I don't want to forget as long as I live: as I pulled back onto the road and the dust kicked up from beneath my tires, I looked in my sideview mirror, and there he was—my new brother—elbows on his knees, *reading his new Bible.*

A man bows before the Spirit of Jesus and launches himself into every adventure and goodness, every value and joy, every fulfillment and wonder, every quality of manliness that a man's life can possibly be.

"The Spirit of Truth," as Jesus called Him. "The Counselor," and oh, how a man needs God's counsel! "The Spirit of God" who leads, protects, and provides . . .

Jesus, Jesus, Jesus. Glory to the Name of Jesus!

A MAN OF GENTLENESS

Some years ago Michael Card wrote and recorded a short, simple song that is the most "Jesus" song I've ever heard: "The Gentle Healer." It's so pure and real, and it captures Jesus in such precious innocence that one gets the sense of how Jesus must have appeared through the eyes of a child two thousand years ago.

As I listen to the melody and lyrics, I picture a little girl going about her precious little life when suddenly this Man arrives in town—this Man everyone is talking about, this Man who does marvelous things. She sees Him in the marketplace where her mom shops, and she watches Him from behind her mom's skirt. Maybe He spies her and gives her a little wink or a nod that sends her behind Mom's skirt even more.

Still, in that little-girl way, she peeks out and watches the Man. She watches Him kneel in the dirt and cry sometimes, holding someone in His arms. She watches Him "fix" those people that others in town always laughed at.

She can see just a hint of tiredness behind the Man's big, big smile. She looks, and she can see the dirt under His finger-nails and the wear in His clothes. She can see that the elbows of His cloak are nearly worn through, and the hem is frayed. Dad would never wear clothes like that; Mom would make him throw them away.

She can see He has thick, calloused hands—just like Daddy's. But what He does with them is so different: *He reaches them into people's pain*. It's such strange behavior for a big person, and yet so breathtakingly wonderful.

Such a strong Man, this Man. So strong and yet so soft. JESUS.

It's an entirely novel thought for a lot of guys: gentleness in masculinity. It so diametrically clashes with our common no-tions of what masculinity is and what masculinity requires. After all, how does a man tenderly tackle the challenges he faces in everyday life? Aren't "tender" and "tackle" complete opposites? Don't nice guys finish last? Isn't softness the hallmark of a sissy?

Think *masculine* and you tend to think of a football player smashing into another football player. A no-nonsense guy marching in and getting what he wants. Victory, attitude, con-trol, dominance—surely these are the makeup of a *real* man.

On the other hand, there's Jesus, the most take-command Guy in universal history. As King of kings, He was the Dominant of dominants. Never has a man marched in more boldly and gotten what he wanted with more determination and guts. Never has a man enjoyed greater victory.

At the same time, to human eyes, never has a man's victory appeared more like defeat. It's funny how that was with Jesus. His way of dominating was to serve. His "marching in" looked more like getting kicked around. His gold medal was the color of blood, and His "getting what He wanted" was *you and me*.

And yes, Jesus "tackled" His opponents. He tackled them head on and took them out big time. He lowered His shoulder of grace; He charged them with every pound-force of care in heaven. He laid into them with love like you and I can't imagine love.

He reached out and cried tears over their ways. He pleaded with them to understand, and pleaded with His Father that they would understand. Then He bled in the sand that they might be saved.

Father, forgive them, for they do not know what they are doing.
—Luke 23:34

My God, my God, why have you forsaken me?
—Matthew 27:46

It is finished.
—John 19:30

He had all the power of the universe at His fingertips. He could have crushed His enemies with just a thought. Instead He hung there. *For them*, He hung there.

JESUS.

That's Jesus in manliness. That's Jesus in His masculine ways. Is there anything more shockingly opposed to our own ways? Is there anything that blows machismo more out of the sky? Is there anything that takes us more to task as men, that seeks to shape us in ways we so desperately need to embrace?

Therefore, as God's chosen people, holy and dearly loved, clothe yourselves with compassion, kindness, humility, gentleness and patience. . . . And over all these virtues put on love, which binds them all together in perfect unity.
—Colossians 3:12, 14

Jesus was gentle, pure and simple. It seems odd to speak of the Son of the living God in such an undramatic way, but He was a kind Man—the kindest of men. He was patient, gracious, and humble in every way. He was a calm Man, slow to speak and ready to listen. His manner was

easy,

strong,

still,

and restrained.

Then there was His touch. Can you imagine Jesus's touch—the touch of the living God in the envelope of a human hand?

Can you imagine the strength in a hand that is both human and divine? Years of carpentry had honed that hand and built its musculature. Years of lifting it in worship to His Father had honed it even more.

Pulsating within his hand was all the power of heaven and earth. It could shatter "gates of bronze" and shred "bars of iron" (Psalm 107:16). But what it chooses, instead, is to reach out in the compassion and care, in the tenderness and mercy, that is *God*. It cradles the most fragile and guards the most helpless. It "gathers the lambs in his arms and carries them close to his heart" (Isaiah 40:11).

Can you imagine that hand reaching toward you? You're actually that close to Him—and He turns. He turns and smiles. He smiles *because of you*.

He reaches to take your shoulder. His hand is rough and calloused, dark and tanned. You can feel its brawn as He wraps around your arm. It could crush, but it doesn't. Instead He enfolds you in safety. Like a waterfall of honey, it spills warmth over your shoulder and massages kindness into your soul.

His eyes beam delight. His smile says, "I love you." The ease of His manner is a fortress of calm. The purity of His goodness breathes healing and care. His affection is beyond whatever you imagined affection could be. It whispers, "I treasure you, My child. Don't be afraid. *I love you*."

JESUS.

There is a remarkable "Jesus encounter" recorded in Luke 7:36–50. It's so intensely personal an encounter, so intimate, so shockingly vulnerable: a woman bathes Jesus's feet in the warmth of her tears; she dries them with her hair; she kisses and kisses them, then bathes them again in precious perfume. My goodness!

JESUS.

She was a broken woman. We have no details that describe her brokenness—only the hint that she had a "reputation" among the men who were there. But the depth of her brokenness was evidenced in her behavior. How broken is a woman that she would cry so deeply, so shamelessly, in the presence of others? How broken that she would drop her face to the dirt and humble herself in such a way? *How broken that she would so desperately seek Jesus?*

I would have to guess there was a time when she was just a happy little girl—like that little girl I imagined in "The Gentle Healer" story. Then something happened. Either something happened to her, or something happened around her, or she made a choice she never should have made. Maybe she was betrayed, or maybe she betrayed herself, or maybe it was a little of both. Maybe someone or something hurt her so deeply and so often that she adopted hurt as her lifestyle.

The possibilities are endless in this far-from-perfect world filled with far-from-perfect people, in which far-from-perfect little girls are forced to live. Whatever the reason, this little girl's innocence was shattered somewhere along the line. Her laughter was silenced. A day turned into years, and now she lies weeping at Jesus's feet.

Can you even begin to imagine such a moment? Here Jesus is sharing a meal with a group of men who literally wish Him dead. No doubt He is simply reaching out to them, loving them. Then suddenly there's this woman.

I don't know what triggered her weeping that day. As I imagine her, she's had so much pain in her life that she's had to learn to bottle it up and cope and carry on. Then, just as something terrible happened so long ago that set all the pain in motion, something wonderful happens that takes it all away. Maybe it's something as wonderful as the presence of the Son of God; and like the pus that flows from a lanced wound, all that pain is released, and the tears just flow.

Had she been watching Jesus for a while, maybe following Him from town to town? Or had she listened to Him for the first time that afternoon, and His words just swarmed her heart? Maybe when she heard Him say "I love you" to people, she knew He really meant it. Maybe when He said, "I tell you the truth," she knew deep inside that He truly was.

Or maybe it wasn't His words that touched her as much as it was His ways. Maybe it was just that He was so shockingly *real*, so kind and caring. When He called her to holiness, He didn't do it in the condemning way so many others did. She didn't feel scolded; it was more like she was being "invited to goodness."

There was joy in His eyes; there was promise of a future! But she could see pain in His eyes too. She could see the pain of a heart that was actually, literally broken over all the hurt in her life and how none of it had to be. Oh, how His eyes whispered to her with such hope and desire! "Be free, My child. Sin no more. Come to Me!"

No words fall from her lips in the presence of Jesus that day. There are no words. There is no "religious formality." There's just *complete and total abandonment of self.* She pours everything out, shamelessly. She withholds nothing from Jesus. She weeps and weeps and weeps.

It was her entire offering to Jesus that day. It was all she had to offer Him, really: her sin and hurt—her "dirt," if you will. Little did she know she couldn't have offered Him anything more "right." "The sacrifices of God are a broken spirit; a broken and contrite heart, O God, you will not despise" (Psalm 51:17). There's *nothing* that could have blessed Jesus more!

She hadn't even begun, however. Having just abandoned herself to Jesus, she abandons herself even more.

She lowers her face.

She unpins her hair.

She cleans His feet with her beauty.

The people gasp. Maybe some of them get upset and even bark at her to stop. But she pays no mind. Jesus is the Lord of her life now, and that's all that matters. Who cares what people think? She belongs to Jesus. She's clean and she's new!

But wait! Just when the onlookers think it is safe to breathe, she lowers her face even more. She cups her hands around His feet. She reaches with her lips (my goodness— no!) *and she kisses them.*

JESUS.

Has there ever been a more beyond-astonishing, beyond-unimaginable scene of repentance and affection, understanding and devotion? This remarkable woman, so breathtakingly vulnerable, so completely broken, so abandoned, so raw. And Jesus, who responds to her in the exact same way He would soon respond while hanging from a tree, to those who were less remarkable, *does nothing*. He just loves her and receives her love. He embraces her affection with calm and respect. He "holds" her in arms of stillness and ease. He cares.

JESUS.

And therein is the key: Jesus *knows* this woman. In the fullness of His divinity that day, He knows her every tear; He knows exactly where each one has come from. He knows every hope His Father ever had for this woman and every hope He continues to have.

For you created my inmost being;
you knit me together in my mother's womb.
—Psalm 139:13

He knows how fragile she is as she lies at His feet. He knows how big this moment is in her life and what it means for her future. He knows how harshly she's been treated, how delicate her emotions are, and how the tiniest gruffness could break her.

So in the fullness of His manhood His response is oh so breathtaking. He does the most extraordinary, most gentle, most tender, most understanding thing a man could possibly do: nothing. He's the Son of the living God, and He allows her to kiss His feet and weep.

JESUS.

It's as if she were a butterfly in the fold of His carpenter hands. The slightest move could injure her—and He knows. The slightest stir, the slightest push or pull could crush her new "wings." "A bruised reed he will not break" (Isaiah 42:3). Jesus.

I can only imagine the softness, the almost-whisper in His

voice as He speaks over her, not wanting to disturb a thing, not wanting to upset her in any way.

"Do you see this woman?" He says to all the "fancy folk" around Him. "I came into your house. You did not give me any water for my feet, but she wet my feet with her tears and wiped them with her hair. You did not give me a kiss, but this woman, from the time I entered, has not stopped kissing my feet. You did not put oil on my head, but she has poured perfume on my feet" (Luke 7:44–46).

He honors her. There she lies, in the narrowness of their human arrogance, a shameful heap and anything but honorable—*and Jesus honors her in front of them all.*

She's come to Him broken of spirit and broken of heart. She's come fragile and without any hope. In manliness beyond manliness, He cherishes her, covers her, and repairs her. He honors, protects, and treasures her. He gently heals her with

quietness,

   dignity,

      and care.

I imagine that a moment eventually comes when Jesus reaches down and lifts her chin so He can look into her eyes. Maybe tears form in His eyes too. Maybe they drip onto the floor right next to hers.

And He smiles. "Your sins are forgiven," He whispers

through that smile. "Your faith has saved you; go in peace" (Luke 7:48, 50).

He was the most gentle of men two thousand years ago. He was "The Gentle Healer."

JESUS.

Glory to the Name of Jesus!

As I type these words today, my father is seventy-six years young. I have to tell you, he's such a treasure to me. I so enjoy him, and being very aware that many folks don't have their fathers, I thank God for him every day.

It wasn't too many years ago that I almost lost him, though. I'll never forget that hospital room and all those tubes and wires and my father looking so helpless.

My father had always been an extraordinarily strong man. He did blue-collar work his whole life and had the forearms to prove it. Truly, I've seen my father tear phone books in half and torque a bolt down so hard it turned into a weld.

The one time he got "physical" with me, I'll never forget. I made the life-endangering mistake of telling my mother to shut up. My father came out of his chair, and with one hand he grabbed me by the collar of my shirt—I was a hefty fifteen years old at the time—and lifted me completely off the ground.

As you can guess, I never told my mother to shut up

again. But that's how strong my father was. So to see him in the hospital looking so seemingly helpless, well, you can imagine . . .

Praise God, the Lord saved my father. But in the middle of that ICU experience, somewhere in the quiet of one of those nights when I sat by his bed, my thoughts wandered to a time years before when the two of us sat together under very different circumstances in the garage of the home I grew up in.

I was maybe in the fourth grade, and one of my favorite places to go with my buddies was the Rexall Drug Store next to the Jack in the Box. We'd all jump on our Sting-Ray bicycles and pedal over there. We'd buy ice cream and bubble gum and read the comic books off the rack till we were chased away. We just *loved* that Rexall Drug Store.

Rexall had a toy aisle, which, of course, was my favorite aisle to roam. I didn't ever have more than a few coins in my pocket, so I couldn't buy anything, but I would walk up and down that aisle and just dream.

There were little green plastic soldiers, model planes, and plastic dinosaurs. There were rubber Gumbys and Pokeys. The entire aisle was like paradise to me. But there in the middle of it lay my biggest toy dream of all: those little tins of Play-Doh. Oh, how I dreamed about Play-Doh and all the cool things I could do with it. What fun I could have—if only I had enough money to buy some!

I have to confess, I wanted that Play-Doh *so, so* badly that one day I decided to (here goes my reputation) steal it. (I know, I know—but God's already forgiven me, so cut me some slack.) In my little fourth-grade head, it seemed like my only option. So one very grim Saturday morning, after hours of meticulous planning, I carefully pedaled my Sting-Ray down to Rexall intent on pulling off my first "caper."

Thinking back, it's so hilarious. I arrived at the store before it even opened. Once inside, I stood in that toy aisle doing nothing for practically *forever*. You must understand, I'd never tried anything like that, and my little fourth-grade heart was pounding right out of my little fourth-grade chest. I was so scared, it's a miracle I didn't soil my dungarees!

Well, in all my scheming, there was one *huge* detail I hadn't figured in: the massive pharmacy window that looked straight down onto the toy aisle. It was elevated, and the pharmacist had a bird's-eye view of everything. So to make a long story short, I was nabbed two steps out the door.

I'll never forget it. I finally made the grab and tucked the tin under my belt. I made a beeline for my Sting-Ray, and with only one leg swung over the saddle, *ka-boom!* This pharmacist's claw came down and grabbed me, and it was over. So much for my criminal career, and so much for my Play-Doh.

The pharmacist was not exactly gracious, I can tell you. In fact, as I remember him, he was about, oh, twenty-eight feet tall and oddly resembled Lurch from *The Addams Family*.

He told me he would call the police and *blah, blah, blah,* and I can remember the tears rolling down my face. I can only praise God that when push came to shove, he decided to simply pick up the phone and call my dad.

That drive home with my dad was the longest in my little-kid history. The Sting-Ray was loaded into the trunk, and not a word was spoken the entire way. I remember Dad talking with the pharmacist before we left, though. I don't remember the exact words—just that the pharmacist was talking tough and all, and my dad pretty much stood quietly and listened. Then we climbed into our old Plymouth and eventually turned into our driveway.

We both headed straight into the garage. That's where our "talks" always took place, so I didn't have to be told. I knew exactly where to go, and I knew exactly where to sit. I knew I'd messed up big time, too, and I knew I was in big, big trouble.

My father sat on an upturned bucket, as was his custom. I felt so bad, I couldn't look him in the eye and just sat staring at the cement floor. A long time passed. Then, ever so calmly, he simply said, "Why would you do something like that?"

There was no anger, no edge in his voice, no intimidation. There was no putting me down, no sense of "How stupid could you be?" My dad spoke so gently, so sincerely that day. The only thing I heard in his voice was deep and genuine care, true and open concern. He asked the question as if he truly wanted to know—as if he wanted to understand his beloved son and what would cause his beloved son to steal.

You'll laugh, but I can remember my answer as clearly as if it were yesterday. I thought and thought, then finally said, "I just wanted it, I guess." My father reached across with one of his huge, calloused paws and rested it on my chubby little forearm. I can still feel the warmth in his hand today. I can still feel the calm and assurance.

He said as softly as a man has ever said anything, "You should have asked me, Bruce. I would have given it to you. You don't have to steal. I love you. Promise me that next time you'll just ask, OK?" He reached up and lifted my face. "Promise me?"

I nodded my little head, and Dad scrubbed my flattop. Then he cupped my face with his other hand and continued, "Let's not tell your mother about this, OK? It'll be our little secret. It's just between you and me."

He smiled and went, "Shhhhhh." I nodded again. He wiped the tear stains from my cheeks, and it was over. I got my Sting-Ray out of Dad's trunk, and I never tried anything like that ever again.

I told that story at a family dinner about six months ago. To my astonishment, my mother was totally surprised. She had no idea. My father had kept his promise all those years. Decades later it was still "our little secret."

That's the kind of man my dad was as I was growing up,

and that's the kind of man he still is today. He had hands that could have crushed me that day—hands that could have beat a kid, or even an adult, black-and-blue. He had forearms that were thick and brawny—*kind of like Jesus's.*

Some would even say he should have given me a good whack or two; who knows. But he didn't. He didn't even raise his voice. When he touched my arm and scrubbed my head, it was nothing but affection and care. With every word he said, with every glance and every pause, it was just "I love you. You're my son, and I love you." My gentle, gentle dad . . .

I never went back to that Rexall Drug Store. But it wasn't too long afterward that I rode my Sting-Ray up the driveway and there was my dad, again in the garage, and he had this big ball of play dough slapped on the workbench next to him. It wasn't Play-Doh brand play dough; it was something he'd gotten from work that was a whole lot better. It was stronger and held together better, and he'd brought it home just for me.

Hey, I was excited! I spent hours and days molding faces and animals and all sorts of stuff. Sometimes he and I would make stuff together too.

The dough was "industrial strength" and kind of gray in color, and man, I had a ball with it. It was so cool, because none of the other kids in the neighborhood had anything like it. Sometimes they'd get a little jealous and ask me about it. I remember puffing up—I was just so proud—and boasting, "Yep, my dad says it's special play dough, not like that junky Play-Doh you see in the store." "Nope, you can't buy it anywhere—it's kind of special." "Where did I get it? My dad got it for me. Yep, my dad . . ."

A man, a father, models Jesus in strength and in gentleness. He cherishes his son. He handles him with care and quietness. He surrounds him with tenderness and builds his little life with warmth and affection.

He says, "I love you" over and over with every touch and in every way. He nurtures his son with ease and kindness and silently breathes "*Jesus*" into the ears of his soul.

Jesus, Jesus, Jesus. Glory to the Name of Jesus!

A Man of Integrity

No book about the person of Jesus or about manhood in general can be complete without turning to the most fundamentally masculine quality of all: integrity.

Integrity is the bottom line of manhood. There is no other reality more basic. It is so breathtakingly central to manhood that there is no "being a man" without it.

Interestingly, a man still can be many other things, though—even good and admirable things. He can be a gifted leader or one who makes great contributions to society. He can be a captain of industry, a great philanthropist, or even the spearhead of a dynamic ministry.

It's wonderful when a man achieves, but achievement is not what makes a man a man. *Character makes a man a man.* And at the core of character is integrity.

Integrity is character's foundation, its cornerstone and capstone. Character is born in integrity and survives in integrity. Take integrity out of a man's makeup, and you've got rubble. Like a house built on sand, everything collapses "with a great crash" (Matthew 7:27).

Two thousand years ago, Jesus stood as a tower of integrity. His integrity was consummate, astonishing, beyond-the-beyond. It rose in Him as high as the clouds, and its magnificence dominated every darkness that sought to slither about His feet.

Can you picture such a tower? Its steel beams of truth crisscross upward as far as the eye can see, rivets of righteousness invulnerably welded into each joint and juncture. No bomb can topple it; no rust can corrode it. No hole is big enough to unseat its foundation.

It's a superstructure of "Let your 'Yes' be 'Yes,' and your 'No,' 'No'" (Matthew 5:37). Designed and constructed by the living God Himself, it's an architectural wonder, mind-exploding in its prowess, breathtaking in its beauty—indeed, the "*splendor of his holiness*" (Psalm 29:2).

Stand at its entryway, and feel the sweet mist that splashes from its fountain of nobility. Wander through its halls and experience living dignity. Step into its courtyard of

value,
>honor,
>>and honesty.

Rest in its garden of faithfulness.

Climb its stairs to the top, where the ground below and all the falsity that crawls over it vanish with glorious distance. Climb to the very top—*and touch the face of God!*

Imagine the Man two thousand years ago. Truth and truth alone flows from His lips. Every word and syllable is a whitewater rush of kingdom purity, a crystalline river teeming with life abundant.

Genuineness and trustworthiness ooze from His touch. To feel His hand in yours is to know the physical reality of certainty and calm. Like warm honey, His brawn wraps around your every doubt and massages peace and security into the most unsure places of your innermost being.

And to look into His eyes—oh, those eyes! From all the way across the hillside or marketplace, He turns and spots you. Of all the people rushing about, you are the focus of His gaze. His arms fall limp to His sides, and He smiles. He dips His head to the side, and His eyes light up. They light up with the joy of knowing you, His precious, precious child; they light up with all the joy and fullness of a Man who is completely true.

Then they whisper. From across the crowd, to you, they whisper. They whisper an embrace of such warmth around your soul—warmth like you never imagined warmth could be.

He draws you into His holiness and "kisses" your heart

through His eyes: "I am your way, My child, and the whole of your life. I am Jesus—your living, breathing, loving Truth!" Glory to the Name of Jesus!

For the lips of a priest ought to preserve knowledge, and from his mouth men should seek instruction— because he is the messenger of the LORD Almighty.
—Malachi 2:7

But Jesus came and touched them.
"Get up," he said. "Don't be afraid."
—Matthew 17:7

Jesus answered, "I am the way and the truth and the life.
No one comes to the Father except through me".
—John 14:6

Jesus, Jesus, Jesus!

Two thousand years ago Jesus said, "Then you will know the truth, and the truth will set you free" (John 8:32). As He spoke those words that day, He stood as a Man who *was* living Truth, and the truthfulness He called men to was a truthfulness that would set them free.

Oh, the hope in His heart that men would live free—

free of foolish attachments,
    free of fear and confusion,
        free of self-pursuit and self-importance!

Oh, that men would live free of all those "lordships" that so entice a man to be less than all a man can be!

Two thousand years ago, Jesus walked with absolutely no obligation to the carrots that lure a man into compromise. He was not fixated on comfort or privilege, security or fortune, the admiration of peers, or getting ahead. There was no "want" in Jesus whatsoever—*other than the want of you and me*. Jesus lived *entirely free*.

There was no such thing as cutting corners, no shaving a little off the top or fudging here and there. Jesus never once had to look over His shoulder or wonder if He did the right thing. He never had to cover His tracks, explain Himself, or not look someone in the eye. In masculine integrity, Jesus lived *entirely free*.

There wasn't one syllable, one gesture, not even one glance that wasn't genuine. There wasn't one commitment that Jesus didn't see all the way through. There wasn't one promise that He didn't fulfill, not one relationship neglected or responsibility shirked, not one day of work "phoned in sick."

With Jesus it was just faithfulness, honesty, forthrightness, honor, candor, loyalty, decency, and principle. Those were the glories that Jesus lived two thousand years ago—the glories of integrity that set a man free.

"Be free, My son," He calls to us all through the tunnel of time. "Come and be gloriously, gloriously free!" Glory to the Name of Jesus!

About the ninth hour Jesus cried out in a loud voice, '*Eloi, Eloi, lama sabachthani?*'—which means, 'my God, my God, why have you forsaken me?' . . . And when Jesus had cried out again in a loud voice, he gave up his spirit" (Matthew 27:45, 50).

We think of the Crucifixion as

> an act of love,
>> an act of grace,
>>> the ultimate sacrifice,

and it truly was all of those breathtaking things. At the same time, it was the most monumental, most all-encompassing, most triumphant and victorious display of integrity in all of universal history. It was, indeed, integrity's greatest hour.

What can you say about a Man who is so faithful to His bride, so loyal to His beloved, so committed to the apple of His eye—*so true to you and me?* He gives His life and He gives His death . . . to you, to me. In full possession of all the might and glory of a thousand universes, He hangs there . . . and He dies.

Hundreds of years earlier He'd spoken a promise—He'd made vows to you and me. "The LORD appeared to us in the past, saying: 'I have loved you with an everlasting love; I have drawn you with loving-kindness'" (Jeremiah 31:3). "I will save you from the hands of the wicked and redeem you from the grasp of the cruel" (Jeremiah 15:21).

Jesus had made those vows and so many more like them. He had promised to save you, and He had promised to save me. He had promised that He'd never abandon us, regardless of how many ways we might abandon Him.

He'd said, "No matter what, no matter *anything*, you, My child, are My world." "You have stolen my heart, my sister, my bride; you have stolen my heart with one glance of your eyes, with one jewel of your necklace" (Song of Songs 4:9).

JESUS.

Hundreds of years earlier Jesus had made those vows; now, hundreds of years later, He spreads Himself across a piece of wood and sees them through. He fulfills them. He lives them out. He "nails Himself" to those vows. He bows His life before them and dies. He dies being faithful. He dies being true.

You see, it's actually very simple to Jesus. He had given us His word. He'd pledged His devotion and promised our rescue. And so He hangs there. He keeps His word. Integrity—unto the very last drop of His precious, precious blood.

"It is finished," He says (John 19:30). "My promise has been kept, My vows fulfilled, My word completed. The debt is paid—*and My beloved is born again!*"

Honor beyond honor; truthfulness stained red. Commitment, responsibility, loyalty, faithfulness; faithfulness to you, and faithfulness to me.

"I told you I'd save you, My child. I told you I love you."
JESUS.

I can only imagine what those six hours must have been like two thousand years ago. No, I can't imagine. No one can imagine.

I can only recall my own mini-horror the day I reenacted those hours on film in *The Gospel of Matthew*. The director strongly emphasized realness as opposed to religiousness, and the miniscule whisper of realness we tapped into nearly drove me to emotional breakdown. That's how horrific that whisper was, in spite of how much I'd prepared.

The story's been told in a previous book and from countless platforms, but there's one thing that happened that day that I've rarely shared. It's an odd detail to consider, especially in the context of such a monumental event.

As I share it here, I want to warn you: your first reaction may be to laugh. It's so bizarre and, as you'll see, so entirely "uncomfortable." At the same time it's so real, so graphic, and frankly, so ugly, that it calls us to more honestly face what truly happened that Golgotha day.

As an actor, I was hanging on that cross from two leather straps. My hands were jammed into those straps, and then they were painstakingly "made up" with prop blood and gore.

That meant my hands were more or less locked in. I couldn't be pulling them in and out, because the makeup would then have to be redone. Once the makeup was completed, my hands had to stay there—for hours.

So there I was "hanging," and the film began to roll. People began screaming murder in my face and spitting at me. I felt the nakedness and the filth, the ache and the strain. It was all so personally terrible—*and I was just faking it*.

In the midst of that horror, something happened that I'd never considered before in terms of Jesus's crucifixion. A fly came and settled on my face. I have to guess it was attracted to all the makeup and gelatin smeared on my skin. People had been spitting on me too; and then there was all the sweat.

The fly crawled all over my face and my neck. It crawled in my beard and into my mouth. It crawled inside my nose. My one eye was glued shut, and the other was glued open, and that fly literally crawled on my eyeball; it just went on and on. I could do nothing. It was awful.

I would like to say I thought of Jesus in those moments, but it took everything I had just to maintain composure. It hit me later that night as I lay in my bed, though. In the dark I stared at the ceiling, thinking through the day and all that had happened. It was then that I remembered that fly. I remembered that fly—*and I thought of Jesus*.

That day, two thousand years ago, Jesus's flesh had been

flayed. His face had been torn beyond recognition. "There were many who were appalled at him—his appearance was so disfigured beyond that of any man and his form marred beyond human likeness" (Isaiah 52:14).

That day, two thousand years ago, there was no flesh. There was no face. There was just caked and clotted blood. There was just (forgive me) raw meat. Is there anything that attracts flies more?

JESUS.

He hung like that for six hours. For six hours His hands were pinned to the crossbeam. Oh, He could easily have exercised one miracle thought and made it all go away—but He didn't. He just hung there . . . and hung there, and the flies crawled in His eyes and in His mouth. I can't imagine their numbers. They crawled in His nose and feasted on His wounds. Hour one, hour two, hour three, hour four . . . They swarmed and they swarmed . . .

JESUS.

For this is what the Sovereign LORD says:
I myself will search for my sheep and look after them.
—Ezekiel 34:11

"Do not be afraid, O worm Jacob, O little Israel,
for I myself will help you," declares the LORD,
your Redeemer, the Holy One of Israel.
—Isaiah 41:14

"For I know the plans I have for you," declares the LORD,
"plans to prosper you and not to harm you,
plans to give you hope and a future."
—Jeremiah 29:11

Hundreds of years earlier, Jesus had given you and me His word. He'd promised salvation and hope, goodness and value. He'd promised joy unto eternity and strength for the day. He'd vowed His devotion and promised His love to the end. He'd said, "Don't worry, little one, I have it all taken care of." And so, hundreds of years later, He hangs there, and the horror comes. He hangs there . . . and He dies.

I think of Jesus those six hours, and I think about all that must have been going through His mind. There He is, in the middle of the most pivotal moment in universal history. He's actually living the fulfillment of all He had guaranteed, "parting the Red Sea" through which you and I would cross to eternal safety, bleeding a red sea in which all our enemies would be drowned.

I think of Jesus just hanging there. It's late in the day, and there's noise swirling all around Him—laughter, crying, coming and going. Shock and numbness have mercifully taken over; He's just still.

His consciousness is dim, and deep within its last remaining chamber, He whispers: "Thank You, Father. Thank You. We made it, didn't We? Yeah, We made it.

"I miss You, Dad. This time away from You has been so hard. I miss You so much. But just look at them, Dad—*they're going to be saved.* Hey, that's so nice. It's so nice that it kind of brings a smile to My—well, You know what I mean . . .

"I love you, Dad. I'll be home soon. It's funny, but in a way I'm going to miss them. I know it sounds crazy, but I just love them so much, and it's been gratifying to actually touch them and hug them and wipe the tears from their eyes. They've given me a lot of trouble, I know. But I love them so much . . .

"Every minute of this day and every minute away from You has been so worth it, Dad. In fact, I can see all their faces lined up in glory. There's Eric just glowing, and Stephanie free from her wheelchair. There's Kathleen, her heart healed and whole. There's Alex, and he's just so full of joy . . .

"Hey, I'd do it all again in a heartbeat, Dad—but thanks, of course, that I won't have to.

"I love You, Dad. I'll be home soon. Take care of them for me for the next few days, will You, Dad? Of course You will.

"I love You, Dad. I love You."

JESUS.

Is all that imagining right or wrong? Who can know? I just know that Jesus was true—true all the way to the end that would be anything but His end.

Oh, the integrity of Jesus—a Man who lived, died, and lived again in genuineness, forthrightness, honesty, and righteousness. A Man who was everything of

> truthfulness,
>> commitment,
>>> honor,
>>>> and faithfulness.

A Man who was everything He preached all men could be.

JESUS!

Do not work for food that spoils, but for food that endures to eternal life, which the Son of Man will give you. On him God the Father has placed his seal of approval.
—John 6:27

Jesus, Jesus, Jesus. Glory to the Name of Jesus!

I have a good friend here in Southern California who enjoys leading a tremendous ministry. Because of a certain level of notoriety he achieved in his secular field a long time ago, he began to get invitations to speak at youth rallies and such; and as God would have it, today he finds himself in full-time ministry. I'm being intentionally vague, because when I asked him if I could tell his story, he said yes, but only if I guarded his identity.

I remember when the ministry began for him. He had not yet formed a nonprofit organization, and people began sending him money anyway. Not a lot of money—just enough to feed a few kids who wouldn't have food otherwise and for him to minister in places where the people couldn't afford to bring him in.

He was like a kid in a candy store every time he found a check in his mailbox. Sometimes he would call me with such wonder in his voice. "You won't believe it, Bruce," he'd gush. "I got twenty dollars in the mail today. Praise Jesus!"

I'll never forget the time he mailed back a check for a thousand dollars. It was from a woman who'd just gone through a divorce. He showed me the check—it was written out to his name—but he sent it back. He told me, "She needs this to rebuild her life." That's the kind of guy my buddy is.

Well, as the ministry grew, he applied for nonprofit status. The government was agreeable, and he was off to the ministry races as a full-fledged nonprofit organization. It's amazing what God does when a guy simply says, "I'll go." Glory to Jesus!

It was maybe three years ago that my buddy needed a new car. He'd made some serious sacrifices for the ministry, and one of them was driving an old Buick till it cried for mercy. I remember it was always coughing and sputtering, and there were oil leaks, the seats were tattered, and parts were always breaking. He even had this big Bondo plaster patch on the passenger-side door where some other car had smacked into it and then taken off. He tried to fix the damage himself, but having never done that sort of thing before—well, you get the picture.

So he needed a car, and to him that meant *praying*. In fact, he just flat-out asked God for a miracle. (In ministry, you hear these kinds of miracle stories all the time.) With his cash flow down to a bare trickle, he just got on his knees and prayed, "Do a miracle, Lord! Do a miracle!"

Days turned into months and, for whatever reason, God never did rise to the occasion. My buddy found a used car that fit his needs and decided to take the plunge.

But here's the thing: before he made the tax-exempt move, he'd sat down with all sorts of leaders and sought counsel. The nonprofit world was virgin territory for him, and he wanted to do it right.

Over and over he was told that the way to go was for the ministry to pay him a tiny salary, and then when he needed certain things like a computer or a car, the ministry would make the purchases, and he would simply get to use them. After all, if the things were necessary for ministry purposes, the ministry should pay for them, right?

As it was explained to him, it's kind of like a pastor living in a parsonage. The church owns the home, but the pastor lives in it. Whether the system is right or wrong is not for me to say; that's just the way things tend to be done.

My buddy heard all this counsel, and he respected the guys who shared it with him. But at the same time, that "way it's done" didn't sit well with him—especially when it came to this car. The rationale made sense, and he could understand the "why" of it in his head. Yes, the car would be used for ministry errands. And it was certainly nothing fancy, so no one could say he was going overboard. Still there was this little "tight spot" in his heart about it—one of those funny, deep-down feelings.

I remember him telling me, "For some reason it just bugs me, Bruce. People don't give me money to buy cars; they give me money to feed the kids. If they knew I was going to buy a car with their money, they never would have given it to me."

That was one side of the fence. On the other side was financial reality. The fact was, if the ministry *didn't* pay for the car, my friend was going to have to dig really deep to pay for it himself. He's one of those guys who won't take on debt, so to buy the car, he would have to dip heavily into savings.

I tell you, my buddy struggled. He prayed and prayed and struggled and struggled. He went back to all those guys who'd counseled him and listened again. All the while he kept pleading with God, "Lord, please give me this miracle."

Finally the "twelfth hour" came, and he had to go get the cashier's check. I remember talking with him that morning, and he was still conflicted. Should he get the check from his personal account or from the bank that handled his ministry account? He struggled to the wire, then he bit his lip, chose to go to his personal bank, and had the cashier write the check. When push came to shove, he paid for the car out of his own pocket.

That wasn't so nice for him. It was probably the most joyless car purchase there ever was. He plunked down the money, drove his new used car back to the office, and went about his day. He was as down as down can be. He felt confused, let down by God, and imprisoned by a seemingly inflated sense of right. At one point he found himself wishing he'd never gotten into ministry in the first place.

One thing about my buddy: he's a "gym rat." He loves working out and always takes his lunch hour in the gym. In fact, that's mostly how we've gotten to know each other. When we're both in town, he and I try to work out together. We just pump the iron and talk about the goodness of God. It's really a wonderful way to share brotherhood.

Well, the day he bought that car, he felt so down that he left his office early and hit the gym just to get away and think things through. I wasn't there that day, but he told me he stood face to face with a wall mirror doing dumbbell curls, working on his biceps and forearms, and just praying and praying beneath his breath: "I don't get it, Lord. Why can't I do things like everyone else? Why do I have to think so stinkin' different?" He was really beating himself up.

Then, in his thoughts, He asked God the "big question":

"I don't get it, Lord. You're a God of miracles, and I asked You for a miracle. *How come I didn't get a miracle?*"

The moment he prayed those words, it was as if his whole heart and mind were flooded with sudden understanding. He told me, "God answered me so clearly and so fast, Bruce, I almost dropped the dumbbells."

The Lord said, "I did give you a miracle, My son. *It's a miracle that a man would buy a car with his own money when he didn't have to.* You could have bought that car with ministry money, and no one would have thought twice. But you didn't. You paid for it yourself. That's a miracle—*a miracle of integrity*.

"Do you see now, My son? Do you understand now who I am and what I'm about? Do you see now that I'm even more faithful to you than you want Me to be?

"I *did* give you a miracle, My son—a much bigger miracle than a free car. *I've made you a man of integrity.*"

My buddy said he was so overcome with emotion that he had to leave the gym. It's kind of ironic now that I think about it, but he said he went and sat in his new car. He sat in his new car and just cried and cried: "I'm sorry, Lord. I'm so sorry. I love You, Father. I love you."

My buddy is still driving that car today, and so far no Bondo. The ministry is thriving—people keep giving, and he just keeps feeding kids and saving souls.

And it's so neat: he just got married to the most gracious

and supportive woman. You should see the two of them sitting side by side in that car. It's got bench seats, and she always slides up next to him as close as she can. Her eyes light up when she sits next to him like that. She's so proud of him and so excited about the man God has grown him to be.

A man asks God to give him a miracle, and God gives Him the biggest miracle of all. He reaches His hand past all that man *thinks* he needs and gives him what every man *truly* needs. He makes him a man of integrity. He makes him a man of character. *He makes him a man like Jesus.*

Glory to the Name of Jesus!

A Man of Love for the Father

As I write these words, it's very early in the morning, and I'm sitting on a quiet, secluded beach. This beach is my "prayer closet." Long ago the Lord showed me to take a kind of "Sabbath" once a week—a day where I "turn everything off" and just be still with Him, praying, resting in Him, seeking Him. This beach is where I come to do that.

I could not begin to share all the ways the Lord has met me in those times, leading me, loving me, and yes, giving me a good "smack" now and then. But I will never forget once seeking His guidance as I faced a specific crossroads, crying out, "What do You want me to do, Lord? What is Your will in this?"

His response was mind-blowing, approach-to-life altering, and as you might expect, from way out in left field. It was as if He said, "My will is that you seek to please Me. Discover what pleases Me in this situation, Bruce—indeed, in every situation—and you've discovered My will.

"What pleases Me, you ask? It's on every page of your Bible, Bruce: mercy, kindness, forgiveness, faithfulness, compassion, responsibility, waiting on Me, trusting Me. Integrity pleases Me, Bruce. Yes, step out in integrity and all of these graces. Apply them specifically in your situation. Walk within them daily. Therein, Bruce, is My good and perfect will." Glory to the living God!

It kind of simplifies the Christian life, doesn't it? *Please the Father, please the Father*—and everything else just falls in line. Oh, that we men would be men, so gloriously single-minded men! Oh, that we men would seek to please *Him*!

This chapter is the most "masculine" chapter, bringing to discussion a man's greatest hope for fullness of masculinity. Its theme is the golden key to all hope and possibility of a man's living life in the fullness of his life's most manly possibilities. It's the key that opens the door to all that's gone before—humility, passion, graciousness, respect: *Jesus lived to please the Father*.

It's so shockingly simple and so blatantly obvious that it's one of those realities we tend to pass by in search of "greater truth," as if there is any truth greater. Jesus didn't pass by it, though—*Jesus lived by it*. He founded His whole life on it. He built everything that He was in character and mission within it,

    through it,

        and out of it.

It was the entirety of His focus and pursuit, His complete and total blueprint for living. He lived purely to please His Father. Everything else was born of that remarkable intention.

It didn't matter who He was standing in front of or what setting He was in. It didn't matter if He was sawing wood in His carpenter shop or hanging from a tree. It didn't matter if He was eye to eye with Judas; His mother, Mary; or thousands upon thousands of truth-hungry souls. Twenty-four hours around the clock, Jesus simply sought what pleased His Father, and then He did what pleased His Father. He did it all the way to Golgotha and then some. Glory to the Name of Jesus!

Oh, breathtaker of breathtakers! Oh, to grasp its enormity and value! *To please the Father*: it is literally the nutshell and sum total of Jesus's entire manhood, power, glory, and goodness. Everything that Jesus was as a Man two thousand years ago flowed out of that singular passion and focus. Oh, how He lived to please His Father—*oh, how He died to please His Father*! Every Jesus moment was lived unto the Father.

There's Jesus on the eve of Golgotha: "After Jesus said this, he looked toward heaven and prayed: 'Father, the time has come. Glorify your Son, that your Son may glorify you'"

(John 17:1). "Father, if you are willing, take this cup from me; yet not my will, but yours be done" (Luke 22:42). "Jesus commanded Peter, 'Put your sword away! Shall I not drink the cup the Father has given me?'" (John 18:11).

There's Jesus in the temple courts: "For I did not speak of my own accord, but the Father who sent me commanded me what to say and how to say it" (John12:49). "But Jesus said to them, 'I have shown you many great miracles from the Father. For which of these do you stone me?'" (John 10:32). Even at the age of twelve: "'Why were you searching for me?' he asked. 'Didn't you know I had to be in my Father's house?'" (Luke 2:49).

"Jesus answered, 'It is written: "Worship the Lord your God and serve him only"'" (Luke 4:8). "'My food,' said Jesus, 'is to do the will of him who sent me and to finish his work'" (John 4:34). "And a voice from heaven said, 'This is my Son, whom I love; with him I am well pleased'" (Mathew 3:17).

Jesus, Jesus, Jesus! Glory to the Name of Jesus!

I often think of Jesus alone on the Mount of Olives, which He so often was. I think of the way He was always slipping off by Himself to that quiet place. I don't know if there's anything more precious than the thought of Jesus in private moments like that. I don't know if there's anything more sacred than Jesus "alone with Dad."

A Man of Love for the Father

Can you fathom

the quietness,
the transparency,
the wholeness,
the oneness?

Is there any reality more holy, more pure, more completed in love? Is there any consideration more intimately wondrous than Jesus "nestling" into His Father's heart?

Oh, the joy and pleasure Jesus must have found in His Father those nights! Can you imagine the refuge His Father was to Him and the understanding and encouragement that surely must have flowed? The hour upon hour of safety and rest?

JESUS.

Letting my thoughts wander, I imagine it's a winter night and Jesus bundles up against the cold. Or perhaps it's summer and He wades through the shallows of a mountain stream. Maybe the moon is bright, illuminating all the beauty that surrounds Him. Maybe it's a night with no moon at all.

Jesus looks up into the panorama of stars that smile upon Him, spilling their joyousness into the reservoir of His soul. He created all of this natural wonder with His Creator hands, and now it has become His refuge. Here He can be quiet. Here He can be still. Here He can talk with His Dad. He so loves His Dad.

JESUS.

There's not a whisper to be heard in any direction. Maybe now and again a breeze kicks up or a squirrel scurries across the grass. Maybe a thrush gets startled and leaps from a bush—and then there's silence, blessed silence.

The world down there at the base of the mount is so busy, and people's hearts can be so hard. They race all over grabbing everything they can get, stepping all over each other. They run around bruising and battering one another, not even knowing it, not even knowing why.

It's all so noisy and soiled and rushed, and there's so much in that world that's broken and contrary. He loves the people and aches for their wholeness, but they just laugh and throw their opinions in His face. It's all so overwhelming sometimes.

Up here there's quiet and calm, though, and more than anything else, the understanding of His Dad. He wraps Himself in the softness of this place. He rests His heart in the cradle of its safety. He breathes . . . It's good to be here.

Jesus tips His head back, and a smile spreads across His face. It's a smile like no man has ever smiled, deep and full. It stretches from one end of the night expanse to the other, from the time before time began to the eternity that has yet to come. It stretches from the Alpha and Omega to the Alpha and Omega. *He smiles into the face of Dad.*

In His soul, Jesus climbs into the sureness of His Father's

lap. He presses all that He is into His Father's embrace. He pulls His Father's Spirit arms tight around His every tiredness,

His every wound,

His every hope,

His every hunger of heart.

Jesus loves His Father. He craves His Father's holiness and rest. He craves His Father's ease and majesty. He craves the quality of His Father's Person, the infinity of His care, the glory of His righteousness, the tenderness of His touch.

You have made known to me the path of life;
you will fill me with joy in your presence,
with eternal pleasures at your right hand.
—Psalm 16:11

Then He prays. The hours come and the hours go, the stars disappear and the sun begins to rise—and Jesus prays.

What was it like—Jesus praying as He did those nights? No one can say for sure. In my own mind I picture Him being very real with his Father. No lofty language or poetic construction. Just quiet communion and deep intimacy . . . transparency and pouring out of heart . . . leaning His every-thing in and leaning His entirety on. Crying at His Father's feet and laughing with Him side by side, worshiping Him, enjoying Him, and pleading for people's souls.

Security,

    confidence,

        excitement,

            and rest.

I picture Jesus those nights, a Man entirely relinquished, entirely sure—kind of like a son just "hanging out" with his dad. I picture Him entirely lost in love, wonder, admiration, and joy. Glory to the Name of Jesus!

And He *needs* His Father so much. He cries with His face to the sand, He needs Him so much—and it's *so* OK for a Man to need His Dad. So He bares His wounds. He cries out all the rejection that's spewed in His face every day and all the heartache He suffers over people who are lost and in pain. "I need You, Dad," He cries. "I need You." His heart is so gapingly open before the Father.

JESUS.

Then there are the hours when Jesus kneels in open-faced awe. He understands His Father like no man can, and He's entirely blown away. Draped over a boulder, face against a tree, pacing, He calls out, "I worship You, Father! I worship You, Dad!"

Jesus in prayer, Jesus before His Father, Jesus in love. It's Jesus in the fullness of holy passion and brimming with kingdom hope. It's Jesus standing beneath waterfalls of glory, promise, strength, and truth. It's Jesus dancing till His feet are sore and singing till His throat is raw. It's Jesus weeping. It's Jesus in wide-eyed wonder. It's Jesus begging His Father *for you and me.*

"*Your* kingdom come, Father; *Your* will be done—Yours and Yours alone. Let it be established and built in every corner of My life, Father, and in everything around Me. It's got to be what *You* desire, Father. Oh, that You would be pleased!

"I need You so much, Father. *All* My needs are *You.* Do with Me as You please. You are My life and My greatest desire. There is nothing for Me but You.

"*Your* kingdom come, Father; *Your* will be done. I love You."

JESUS.

One of the neatest little passages in all the Gospels is one that tends to go entirely unnoticed. It's comprised of two short sentences—John 7:53 through 8:1—that on the surface seem more like a bridge between two events than anything of significance. It's one of those little gospel details that a guy reads over and passes right by. Then one day he "sees it" and falls to His face in wonder.

Jesus is in the thick of the Jerusalem battle. He's in the temple area reaching out, and giving Himself, and everything is coming at Him. These people over here are calling Him a demon; those people over there are challenging His every word. There are arguments all around Him, and pushing and shoving. Temple guards even show up to arrest Him.

The day finally comes to a merciful end, and I can't even begin to imagine how exhausted and weary of heart Jesus must have been. This is where the two sentences come in. They read, "Then each went to his own home. *But Jesus went to the Mount of Olives.*" The passage continues with the first few words of John 8:2: "*At dawn* He appeared again."

JESUS.

Here are these mere men with their high talk and religious opinions, assuming their self-righteous selves to be superior in knowledge and understanding. They bark and pontificate, then return to their happy little lives. They suppose themselves so "together" in God, but they hardly give Him the time of day.

Then there's Jesus—a Man who *is* God. If there's anyone in the crowd who "knows His stuff," it's Jesus. If there's anyone who can claim understanding, it's Jesus. If there's anyone who has a right to retire to the comforts of a home, it's Jesus. But He doesn't. Instead He goes to His Father. He returns to bow Himself once again. He returns to seek His Father's face. He returns to give Himself up afresh, again and again.

JESUS.

I picture Jesus on His face that night, begging His Father for those men's souls. I picture Him crying out all the hurt they threw at Him and asking His Father to sooth and heal. I picture Him leaning in: "O Father, O Father . . ."

JESUS.

After the longest time, perhaps, He sits back and takes a long, deep breath. He wipes the soil from His cheek and rises to His feet. He crosses to the edge of the mount, gazing out over Jerusalem below. He turns His thoughts ahead to the next challenge, the next adventure, the next glory, the next joy.

"What do You want Me to do tomorrow, Dad?" Jesus asks. "What will please You?"

In response, the Majesty of all majesties, faithful and sure, gentle and strong, looks upon His precious Son and rises from His heavenly throne.

He's the Ancient of Days,
> the Glory of the Universe,
>> the loving Father.

He bends to gather His Son into the fold of His delight. He smiles—oh, what a smile! He whispers to Jesus, and through the tunnel of time, He also whispers to you and me . . .

"I love You, My Son. I love You. Keep right on leaning into Me, My Son, so that You may walk in My glory and live in My fullness. Seek Me with all Your heart. This is what will please Me, My Son. This is what I want You to do.

"You know who You are in Me and every good purpose for which I birthed You. Be gracious; be gentle, faithful, and true. Go right back out there and pursue them with all that

You are. Humble yourself before them, serve them, and reach out. Continue to cry tears before them; continue to stand for what's right and true.

"You are excellent, My Son—truly excellent. I purposed You for excellence, and You have so valiantly pursued it.

"Hear me well when I say this, My Son. Take it deep into Your heart: *I'm so proud of You.* My heart leaps to think of You. You're a Man who gives Me joy. You're a Man who gives Me pleasure.

"In You I am well pleased, My Son. 'I AM' Your Father, and 'I AM' well, well pleased. I love You, My Son. I love You, I love You, I love You . . ."

JESUS!

As we turn the corner toward conclusion, in lieu of a real-life story, I feel what we really need is to turn our eyes solely toward Jesus. If what I've written in these pages has challenged you half as much as it has challenged me, then we've both got our work cut out for us. Men are challenged to Christlikeness in manhood; women are invited to fresh understanding of what a man truly needs to be. All of us, men and women alike, are challenged to understand Jesus afresh, to fall in love with Him more and more, and to grow in closeness to Him.

It's all so exciting and all so wide open and available. "You will seek me and find me when you seek me with all your heart" (Jeremiah 29:13). And all that "work" that we have cut out for us is really the free gift of His continuing grace. "Until now you have not asked for anything in my name. Ask and you will receive, and your joy will be complete" (John 16:24). Glory to Jesus!

If I may talk with just the guys for a moment, I want to say: *You can do it.*

I'm not "there" yet, and I'm guessing you're thinking the same thing about yourselves. But in the power and certainty of His bigger-than-anything, you and I can do it. We can plant ourselves in the confidence of His hope for us as men and His unquestionable desire to mold us into His likeness of manhood. We can plant ourselves firmly against everything that would pull us away, distract or diminish, or cause us to give up and "go back."

Stand firm in Him, brother. Rivet your gaze on Him, bind yourself with Him, force yourself to choose as He would choose.

JESUS.

Keep in mind that what's been explored in these pages is far from exhaustive. Volumes could be written about the character of the Man, Jesus, and we'd never come close. At the same time, we've gotten off to a start! So let's go for it, guys. Let's refuse anything less than all of Him in every corner of our lives. Let's pursue Him with all of our hearts. Let's rest in His faithfulness to do that which He undoubtedly desires to do. Let's rise from the shackles of doubt, unworthy pursuits, fixations, and excuses—*and then step out into the world!*

We step out into our relationships and workplaces as men "dressed" in Jesus. We step out into our homes and families and every corner of conflict or challenge that this broken world throws our way. We step out into our own hunger for goodness and peace, joy and adventure, the way we know God intends for our lives to be both inside and out. We just step out—*and be men like Jesus.*

We move in gentleness and integrity, humility and grace. Guard your tongue—yes, you can do it! We

> support and care,
>> protect and respect,
>> cherish and honor

the women God has put in our lives. We honor God, too, no matter what it costs; He promises He will never let you or me down. We seek God's Spirit in sensibility and calm. We seek God's Spirit within His Word and build our lives on the sureness of His leading.

You *can* resist that thing that seems to own you. You *can* make a commitment, and you *can* see it through. You *can* be entirely, totally free and become everything in manliness your heavenly Father birthed you to be.

Oh, guys, let's not just talk about Him and go to church and sing the songs. Let's move out into the places and situations of our private and public lives, our families and relationships, and be *real* men. God's got such an incredible plan! And yes, He's even going to take care of "that"—whatever "that" is in your life or mine—which today seems so impossible. It's all so wide open before us. *Let's be men like Jesus.*

When I was a child, I talked like a child,
I thought like a child, I reasoned like a child.
When I became a man, I put childish ways behind me.
—1 Corinthians 13:11

Glory to the Name of Jesus!

Oh, how all of us—men, women, kids, grannies, whomever—need to fall on our faces and cry out harder and seek God more and more! He truly is the end-all of end-alls; oh, how we all need to just "give up" and let go, trust Him, and cast ourselves upon Him! How we need to desperately embrace Him, as He so longs to deeply embrace us!

It's really just a matter of submission, surrender, and dying to self. It's that Gethsemane offering over and over that Jesus cried out so long ago: "Not My will, Dad, but Yours be done." Sure, we can look for a hundred different religious "hooks" or spiritual fast-food fixes to try to squirm out of it, but at the end of the day there it stands as the only way: His way. In character, in circumstances, in relationships and pursuits, His road is the only road that leads us straight to becoming everything we can be—everything He desires us to be.

So join me, will you? Let's get on our faces before Him together. Let's cast all our nonsense at His no-nonsense feet, and do the only thing there is to do:

adore Him,

treasure Him,

and love Him.

JESUS.

I would be remiss if I ended this book without stepping aside and talking with those who have yet to begin a personal life in Jesus. I've obviously written this book guessing that most folks who read it have begun that life already. If that's not your case, I want to "pull over" for a moment and speak to you personally.

Whoever you may be, no matter your background, religious history, or anything else, Jesus longs to live in your heart. He longs to forgive you for your every sin and mistake —the same sins and mistakes we've all made as broken people in a broken world—and bless you freely with eternal life. He longs to begin a wondrous relationship of Him living in you and you living in Him, today and forever unto eternity. Glory to His Name!

He offers Himself freely to you—free for the asking. That's

what it means when you say, "Jesus, come into my heart." There's no magic in that phrase. It's just a way of expressing your desire for Him and your desire to give the entirety of your life over to Him and His Lordship. It's a phrase that says, "Jesus, free me from all my sin. Be my Savior. Close that gap between me and my heavenly Father. I want You in my life. I want You in my life!" Amen and amen.

In these pages, you've read and hopefully realized who Jesus truly is. Perhaps your heart has been touched and stirred. If so, that's simply His "whisper" to you that you might come to Him. That even right now, this very moment, you might join me and cry out to Him from the bottom of your heart, "I want You, Jesus. I want You in my life. Give me new life." If those words express your heart's desire, pray them with me, will you? *"Jesus, come into my life."* Glory to the Name of Jesus! And again, amen and amen!

Whether you've walked with Jesus for fifty years or fifty seconds, I want so much for you to know: *He loves you.* Oh, precious one, let that sink deep into every corner of your soul. *He loves you, He loves you, He loves you.*

JESUS.

He's the Son of the living God. His name is Goodness, Gentleness, Passion, Kindness. His Name is Faithfulness,

Truth, Care, and Devotion. His Name is Understanding and Holiness—and He loves you.

JESUS.

Oh Lord, this precious one is in Your remarkable hands. You love him so much—You love her so much.

I've tried so hard in these pages to make You real, and this has been such a long, incredible journey. How I yearn to reach through these pages and take this reader in my arms and look him or her in the eye and whisper, "He loves you."

I know that's a silly thought, Lord. But if that's how I feel, I can only begin to imagine how You must feel. You love this one so much and desire so much for him, for her—for me too.

Hold this one in Your gracious arms, Lord. Cradle his or her soul. Guard this dear one from every intrusion that would seek to steal any measure of all that You desire for him, for her. Draw this man close to you—he so needs You. Draw this woman close—she so needs You too.

And mold us guys, Lord. It's so beyond wonderful to consider! Make us men who desire and long for and set our focus on becoming men like You.

Father, there's a man reading this page, and You're speaking to him in the private places of his life. You're showing him things, bringing things to the surface.

Maybe his wife is yearning for gentleness, or maybe his children are longing for leadership. There are so many scenarios, Lord, and the astounding reality is that You have Your eyes of hope on every one of them. No man is a lost cause. No man is incapable of being like You. We need only to seek. Glory to the Name of Jesus!

So bless this man, Lord. Bless this precious woman too. I don't know what her situation is, but I do know one thing: she needs You, You, and more of You. Shower her with goodness, Lord. Startle her with loveliness. Love her, Lord. Yes, that's it—love Your precious daughter.

Finally, Lord, for myself, make me a man like You. Build me in Your hope. Reconstruct my character. Put blessing on my tongue and give birth to greater hunger for righteousness. I love You, Lord. I love You. Amen and amen.

Come to me, all you who are weary and burdened, and I will give you rest. Take my yoke upon you and learn from me, for I am gentle and humble in heart, and you will find rest for your souls.
—Matthew 11:28–29

"Come to Me, come to Me, come to Me . . ."
"I love you, I love you, I love you . . ."
Jesus, Jesus, Jesus!

Also by
Bruce Marchiano

"It is appropriate that Bruce Marchiano, who spent so much time and imagination understanding and portraying the 'smiling' Jesus in his powerful film, should now teach us about the Jesus who also wept."

MICHAEL CARD—Author, *Come to the Cradle*; Music Artist

"It's my prayer, and I know, Bruce's passion, that Jesus Wept *will draw you into the Scriptures where you'll hear for yourself the beat of His heart."*

KAY ARTHUR—CEO and Cofounder, Precept Ministries International

Available Where Good Books Are Sold
www.howardpublishing.com